# Watch Over This Vine

## The Weinstein Family's Odyssey of Faith and Survival

NECHAMIE MARGOLIS

People shown in the photographs are identified
left to right unless indicated otherwise.

Copyright © 2020 Nechamie Margolis

All rights reserved. No part of this book may be reproduced or transmitted in any form or by any means, electronic or mechanical, including photocopying, recording, or by any information storage and retrieval system without the written permission of the author.

Library of Congress Control Number: 2020919246

Written and produced by Nechamie Margolis

www.WritingtheSoul.net

Set in Arno Pro by Raphaël Freeman MISTD, Renana Typesetting

אֱלוֹהֵים צְבָאוֹת שׁוּב נָא הַבֵּט מִשָּׁמַיִם וּרְאֵה
וּפְקֹד גֶּפֶן זֹאת.
– תהלים (פ:טו)

🙰

O God of Hosts, return now; look from heaven and see,
and watch over this vine.
— PSALMS (80:15)

This book is lovingly dedicated לעילוי נשמת
our dear parents, grandparents and great
grandparents, the crown of our family:

Rav Chaim Yair HaKohen, הי״ד
& Esther ז״ל Weinstein

❦

הרה״ח הקדוש ר׳ חיים יאיר הי״ד
בן הרה״ח ר׳ משה אריה הכהן ווינשטיין, ז״ל

וזוגתו

מרת אסתר ז״ל
בת הרה״ח ר׳ אלכסנדר דוב פרלמן, ז״ל

# Preface

Since I was a child, I have heard small bits and pieces of the story of my father's escape from the Nazis, *yemach shemam*, before and during the Second World War. I was always curious to know the full narrative and how it corresponded to the historical timeline of the war.

Surely this story impacts me to this day.

The Holocaust has always haunted me, as I'm sure it does most of us. It particularly interests me because of the fact that it deeply impacted my own immediate family. It always felt strange not having had the opportunity to have met my own grandparents. I was always intrigued about them because we are who we are because of who came before us. We stand on their shoulders. We are heirs to a rich tradition of Torah and Chassidus and inherited tremendous spiritual wealth due to the enormous self-sacrifice of the subjects of this book, my grandparents, Rav Chaim Yair and Esther Weinstein.

For years I have had a desire to compile my family's story but being busy with family, work and community it just never got done.

Perhaps it was a Chabad on Campus trip to Poland in March 2017 where I had the privilege of leading a group of sixty college students, along with my two oldest daughters, Esther and Shifra, that made me finally take action. That experience was very profound and I found a possible record of my grandfather's name in the records of Auschwitz-Birkenau.

I also believe that in a world where Holocaust denial exists, every Holocaust story must be documented. This is why copies of this volume will be submitted to the United States Library of Congress, Yad VaShem and other universities and libraries where researchers study the holocaust.

I want to express my deep appreciation to Nechamie Margolis of *Writing the Soul* for researching, interviewing and writing this story and for being such a pleasure to work with. Our family will be forever grateful to you.

Thank you to the editor Chava Dumas for her eye to detail of names and historical events, and her contribution of suggestions during the final editing.

Thanks very much to those who agreed to be interviewed for this project: Malka Greenzweig, Boruch Katz, Alexandre Speaker, Jacqui Sussholz, my father Rabbi Naftoli Weinstein, and Meir Weinstein.

Thanks to Boruch Katz for graciously sharing his research which gave us a great head start, and for his assistance throughout.

I am very grateful to those who provided financial support to help make this book a reality: My parents Rabbi Naftali and Sherry Weinstein, Yair Zvi (Hershy) and Yitty Greenzweig, Akiva and Esther Sussholz, Chanina and Simcha Sussholz, Jacqui and Evie Sussholz, Manuel and Eleanor Sussholz, and Sruli and Malky Weinstein.

Thanks to Rivka Goldblatt of *Jewish Family Research* for the genealogy research.

Thanks to my father, Rabbi Naftali Weinstein, Malka Greenzweig and Boruch Katz for reviewing the manuscript for accuracy.

Thanks to my parents, Rabbi Naftali and Sherry Weinstein, for all they have done and continue to do for me and my family. I feel blessed to have parents who have modeled how to experience some of life's most difficult challenges and emerge with enormous resiliency and passionate *ahavas Hashem, ahavas haTorah and ahavas Yisroel*. I love you very much. May Hashem bless you with many more years in good health and with tremendous *nachas* from your beautiful family.

Thanks to my wonderful wife, Naomi, for being an amazing partner and friend. Her ongoing support and encouragement allowed me to focus on this project.

Thanks to my dear children, Esther, Shifra, Sarala, Leah and

Menachem for being awesome and for supporting my pursuits, including this one.

Thanks to my Rebbe, the Lubavitcher Rebbe, for teaching me how to experience Yiddishkeit and life in an incredible way.

Most importantly, thanks to the Aibishter for ensuring the survival of our family so that we are here today and can serve Him joyfully.

This volume is dedicated to the patriarch and matriarch of our family, Rav Chaim Yair HaKohen, הי״ד and Esther Weinstein, ז״ל. Our large and beautiful family, *bli ayin hara*, is a testament to who they were. From this one couple, who experienced one of the darkest times in human history, emerged hundreds of descendants in all of the wonderful diverse communities that make up *Klal Yisrael* today around the world. They will surely have what to smile about when we all greet them with the coming of Moshiach, may it be immediately.

*I'd love to hear your feedback on this book.*
*I can be reached at aviweins@gmail.com.*

Avraham Chaim (Avi) HaKohen Weinstein
Elul 5780 · September 2020

# Contents

| | | |
|---|---|---|
| Preface | | vii |
| Family Tree | | xii |
| 1. | When the Skies Cried Blood | 1 |
| 2. | The Runaways | 11 |
| 3. | Remembering the Forgotten | 17 |
| 4. | Montesquieu: When War Is Just a Dream | 23 |
| 5. | Gurs: The First Rung of Purgatory | 31 |
| 6. | Aix Les Bains: The Beauty and the Beast | 43 |
| 7. | D'agde: The Night When Angels Come | 61 |
| 8. | Knocking on Heaven's Door: *From Château de Masgelier to Montpellier Hospital* | 73 |
| 9. | From Castle to Cabin: Nantes-en-Ratier | 85 |
| 10. | A Tiny Light in Colombière | 95 |
| 11. | "Who, Being Loved, Is Poor?" | 129 |
| 12. | Passage in the Night | 139 |
| 13. | When the Eternal City Crumbles | 149 |
| 14. | Haven: Sailing Out the Storm | 167 |
| 15. | Land of the Free | 181 |
| 16. | Rising from the Dead | 195 |
| Epilogue | | 209 |
| Maps | | 210 |
| Appendix I – Sources | | 213 |
| Appendix II – Documents | | 215 |
| Appendix III – Document Translations | | 227 |
| Appendix IV – Immigration Records | | 237 |

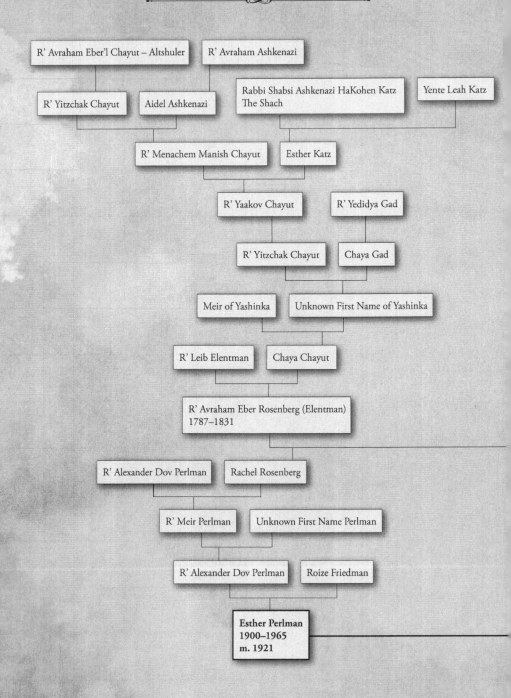

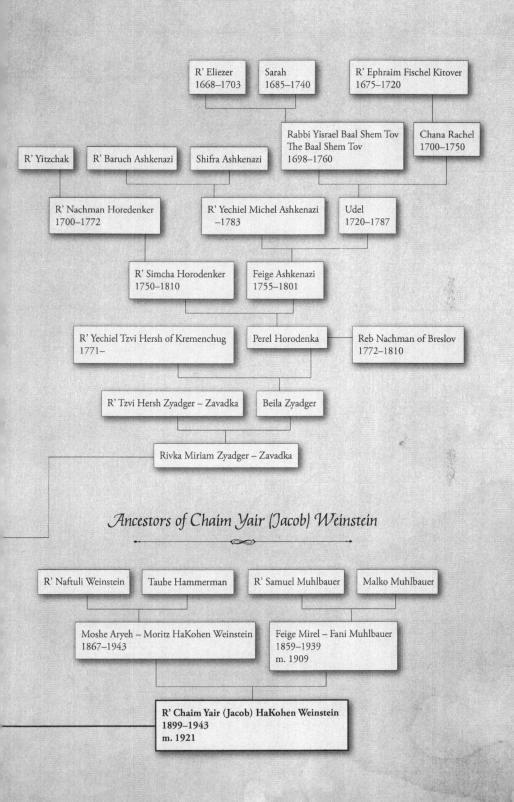

# Current Descendants of Esther Weinstein (Perlman) & Chaim Yair (Jacob) Weinstein

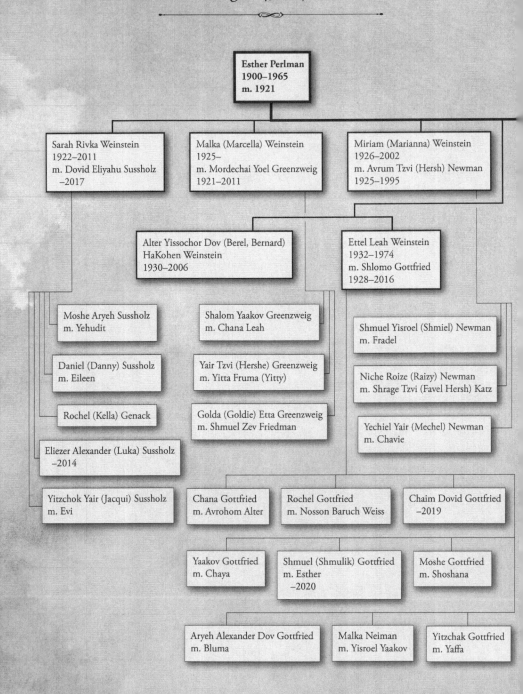

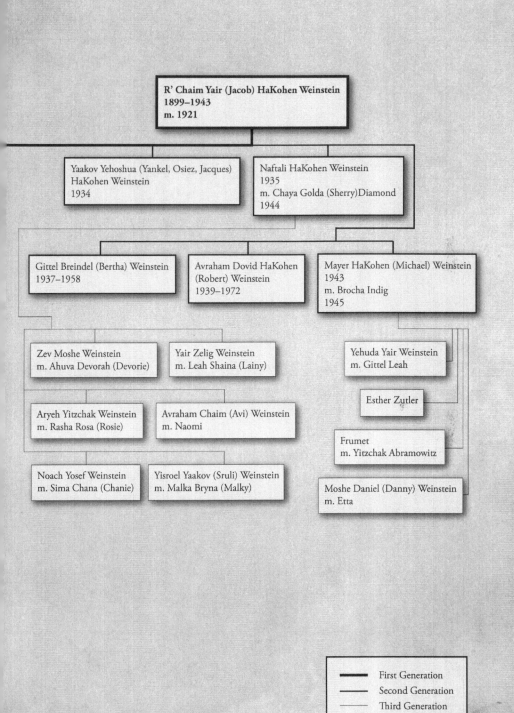

CHAPTER ONE

# When the Skies Cried Blood

MAY 1940

On Lange van Ruusbroecstraat 37, the Weinstein family was peacefully asleep in their spacious apartment in one of many buildings forming the dense labyrinth of the Jewish quarter in Antwerp.

Like a toddler walking on an unprotected precipice, completely defenseless, woefully innocent and completely oblivious of the imminent danger, the Weinstein family was enjoying one last moment of sleep. They were immersed in their pleasant dreams while intensifying thunderbolts and flashes of fiery images stormed outside. One bomb fell only a few blocks away, an earthquake waking the rumbling volcano and sending clouds of ash and fire into the dying night.

Esther and Chaim Yair were jolted awake. What were those terrifying sounds outside? Were they in the midst of the nightmare memories that lingered in their memories from the war of their childhood, images that periodically emerged to torment them? Or was this that dark shadow that had existed for many months now, and in one flash of history, it had entered their present life? Was this a war that was happening now?

Early that Friday morning, May 10, 1940, Captain David Strangeways of British Expeditionary Forces, stationed in Lille in Northern France, was woken up by the battalion orderly shouting, "David, sir, David!"

Dismayed at first for being called by name, Captain Strangeways shuddered. "David" was the code word they were dreading hearing for nine months, since last September.

"David" meant that the German invasion of the Lowlands had begun.

In Antwerp, a hundred miles to the north-east of Lille, barely an hour before, dawn was breaking. The misty half-light was crawling in, chasing the darkness away. These last hesitant moments of the night were slipping into the past, clearing the way for the sun to usher in a new day. Suddenly, as if out of nowhere, the horizon started collapsing, crashing down like in a violent car crash, like a torn aorta of planet Earth pumping out loud bursts of blood, spilling across the sky with an accelerating tempo of explosion. Boom, boom, boom!

German Luftwaffe roamed the skies unchallenged, shedding blinding pyrotechnics of death and destruction. Eleven hundred German fighter airplanes were matched by the exact same number of fighter planes of the Allies, which would have resulted in protracted and deadly air dogfights with no certain outcome. However, four hundred of the Allied bombers didn't stand a chance against the one thousand and one hundred horizontal bombers that the German Luftwaffe boasted. Plus, the Allies had no counterpart for the three hundred and twenty-five German dive bombers, the latest military development. These were the planes that rained German fire and fury on Antwerp that morning.

The Germans had fought against Antwerp in the past. In 1914, after a long and exhausting siege they succeeded in breaking the city. But then, after a few years of trench battles that turned Europe into one massive, muddy dugout filled with bodies, they lost that war, the Great War. Germans were defeated, humiliated and forced to pay reparations, effectively subjected to abject poverty. But now they had returned for revenge, hungry for blood, for restitution. They charged at complacent, laid back Europe with one burning desire: to show everyone that after that bitter defeat, Germany was the ultimate undead, that Deutschland would arise from the ashes and become again *uber alles* – Germany above all!

Germany was about to repeat history, on an even more epic

scale than before, with even more blood, and even more devastating, unimaginable defeat.

But no one knew the future, what was really about to happen. On that fateful Friday, May 10, 1940, after a long military standoff and desperate, frequently cynical, and ultimately failed attempts at political appeasement, Germany was about to shock the world.

※

Beyond the Weinstein's windows lay Antwerp at four o'clock in the morning, careening into a war that would prove to be the greatest and darkest tragedy in human history.

They froze for a moment, then forgetting all caution ran to look out the window. They witnessed a sky set afire, shattering, exploding. Quickly, they woke up their older daughters, sixteen-year-old Sarah, fifteen-year-old Malka, and fourteen-year-old Miriam. Then they woke up their younger ones, ten-year-old Berel, eight-year-old Leah, six-year-old Yankel, four-year-old Naftoli, and three-year-old Gittele. They rapidly rushed to line everyone up, one after the other, to crouch down in the dark narrow stairs that led into the basement.

Esther carried her one-year-old Avraham Duvid clutched close to her, cowering in the shadows. Minutes were slipping away, turning into hours. Then an uneasy, ominous silence descended. They gingerly clambered upstairs, their home miraculously intact, so far undamaged.

But was it safe, and if yes, for how long?

※

The new day brought an uncertainty that crept upon them, as if they were on death row, when the date for the execution was not yet determined. They were facing the unknown, with the awareness that their present moment could be their last one, and this weighed heavily upon them.

Radios across the city flicked on in a desperate attempt to grasp at the straws of breaking news, of clarifications, or some form of directive from those who were supposed to know what they were supposed to do.

But the radio was silent. So instead began the feverish, speculative discussions of desperation with neighbors, with family members. When a great long shadow is cast upon you, what are you to do?

A few days of trepidation passed and Shabbos was approaching. Esther cautiously sent her daughter Malka out to buy challahs. On her way there she met her friend Rifka.

"I don't know what will be with us," Malka began. Though she was only fifteen, she already carried the weight of responsibility that comes with being the second oldest in a large family.

"We never know what will be with us," Rifka responded. "Hashem is here. Don't worry."

But Malka did not feel reassured. Her friend Rifka was from a wealthy home, unlike her own family that was barely scraping by. They owned a car, a luxurious symbol of status in the days of peace and prosperity, a rare opportunity in the days of war. Rivka's family had a chance to escape, a way to flee the approaching German army bearing down on them. This could potentially mean the difference between life and death.

Nothing could stand in the face of massive German tanks, an iron fist of ten Panzer divisions boasting a total of two thousand and seven hundred tanks, rumbling across Belgium. There were bridges built on the go by German engineering corps, planes raining untold scores of parachuting Germans overrunning the countryside and scattered towns, infantry slogging along in terrifying numbers.

The newest German invention of modern warfare, an orchestrated onslaught of all military branches at once, was best manifested in the most updated tactics of the time – close aerial support of ground troops bolstered by air-to-ground radio communications, which the Germans had perfected in pre-war maneuvers and Polish and Norwegian campaigns.

In the future, when historians would view the propaganda

documentaries that Germans filmed while on the roll, to raise the spirits of the German folks back home, they would see that there were squadrons of warplanes swarming the skies and dropping incalculable amount of munitions, massive Howitzer cannons rolling up to their positions, loaded and firing and recoiling on a repeat, ravaging entire neighborhoods. And simultaneously, German troops rowing in rubber boats across the canal, while others were dismounting their bicycles, drawing their rifles from behind their backs and taking positions on the high riverbank. Germans fought with all they had, from the most sophisticated military aircraft of the time, to bicycles. Their goal was to overwhelm their enemy from all directions, in every conceivable way. That was the novel concept of a modern warfare that took Europe by utter shock, the Blitzkrieg, the "lightning war."

But maybe more than the new tactics of warfare and modernized military arsenal, Germans had one massive advantage over their rivals: they formulated a new concept, *Auftragstaktik*, the "mission-oriented leadership." They came to win, and did all they could to achieve that.

The Allied forces, on the other hand, came mentally and strategically unprepared. French tanks, three thousand total, were stretched along the frontline, in one row, an exact replica of the military formation during the Great War a quarter century before, thus making themselves vulnerable to a concentrated assault of Panzer armored groups that formed on the ground as a metaphorical clenched iron fist breaking through whimsy cardboard.

At the outset of World War II, the Allies attempted to fight not the war that they were facing, but the previous one, with outdated tactics and moreover, outdated perceptions of what this war was going to be like. When they finally realized what was happening, it was almost too late.

In August 1939, Lord Thomas Inskip, the British Minister of Defense Coordination, reassured the British public that, "the war is not only not inevitable, it's unlikely." Nine months later, on the eve of Fall Gelb, the German invasion of the Low Countries, despite all Germany had endeavored to state clearly, it seemed that no one was interested in heeding the warning signs. The Belgian army increased the official leave days for its conscripts from two to five days a month, and as many as fifteen percent of the French frontline troops were on home leave. Considering that merely a month prior to that Germany invaded and captured with lightning speed Norway and Poland, this complacency spoke volumes to how mentally unwilling the Allies were to face their enemy. The morale factor clearly was on the wrong side of history.

The only one bright spot on that exact fateful Friday, May 10, proved to be an event of a very different nature, barely noticeable at first glance, a little political shift that took place in a distant place. One Winston Churchill, a man uncharacteristically reclusive for a politician, who, also uncharacteristically for a politician, staunchly held the principled and deeply unpopular view that Great Britain had to fight Nazi Germany, was sworn in as a new Prime Minister of the United Kingdom. He proved to be a man who would stand up, virtually alone, against the popular opinion at home, to the Nazi beast that devoured the entire European Continent.

After most continental European countries surrendered to Germany while others stuck to observing strict neutrality, for a long year Great Britain was the sole enemy and military target of Nazi Germany.

Soviet Foreign Minister Vyachleslav Molotov signed a non-aggression pact with his German counterpart Ribbentrop in exchange for partition of Poland between Soviet Russia and Nazi Germany, thus securing German eastern flanks. The United States, due to political climate and deeply isolationist sentiment, made sure to sidestep the war. Only a long year later, in June 1941, the Soviet Union was dragged into the war after Germany broke their non-aggression pact and launched an assault on Russia. The US followed suit only half a year later, not before the Japanese attacked Pearl Harbor on December 7, 1941.

But between June 1940 and June 1941, the UK stood alone, led by one man. On May 13, three days after he was sworn in as Prime Minister, Churchill had these ominous words to say, as stern as they were candid. Since then they became some of the most famously courageous words ever spoken in modern history: "I would say to the House, as I said to those who have joined this Government: I have nothing to offer but blood, toil, tears and sweat. We have before us an ordeal of the most grievous kind. We have before us many, many long months of struggle and of suffering. You ask, what is our policy? I can say: It is to wage war, by sea, land and air, with all our might and with all the strength that G-d can give us; to wage war against a monstrous tyranny, never surpassed in the dark, lamentable catalogue of human crime. This is our policy. You ask, what is our aim?

"I can answer in one word: It is victory, victory at all costs, victory in spite of all terror; victory, however long and hard the road may be, for without victory, there is no survival."

Absent this solitary, unlikely hero that Winston Churchill proved to become, a man who, ironically, was promptly voted out of office as soon as the war was over, human history would not have been the same.

In Antwerp, on that day, those simple lives were crushed and mangled. Malka's friend Rivka, her family being one of the select enviable few who had cars, did what all the elites did: they drove to the seaside in De Panne, the safest place the Belgians knew ever since the previous Great War.

Like most of those in Europe, they made a fatal mistake by fighting the last war, not the one they were facing. They thought they were lucky, as they whisked off to safety at an unmatched speed of forty miles per hour, thinking that no one would intentionally target civilians fleeing the battlefield. But Germans had a whole different take on this. Europe, all of it, was at fault for their humiliation and misery, and Europe in its entirety had to pay.

As Rifka's family drove away, suddenly a bomb exploded nearby and the shrapnel penetrated the car and killed Rifka's brother. They pulled over and stopped, then turned around and drove back to the mayhem of Antwerp under bombardment, driving for hours with the bloodstained lifeless body of their beloved boy, to bury him at their family plot in the old cemetery of his hometown on that blood splattered Friday afternoon.

When Malka heard this sorrowful news, the tragic irony struck her.

Poverty had kept her family from escaping, cowering down; and yet poverty saved them, at least for that moment.

"You never know," her friend had said.

※

Reb Chaim Yair Weinstein was a devout Belzer *chassid*. He consecrated his entire life to love and fear of G-d, the cultivation of *bitachon beHashem*, absolute trust in the Almighty, under all circumstances, no matter what. The first three years of his married life he spent in Belz near his Rebbe, studying and immersing himself in the world of Torah and *avodas Hashem*. With all his being he delved into the depths of purity and G-dliness.

His eyes, a mirror of the soul, gleamed with the mystery of the unknown he must have touched upon during infinitely long nights devoted to study. His face, as if chiseled from white marble, with high cheekbones and towering forehead, adorned with a full black beard, represented his total belonging to the paths of the forefathers. He himself looked like he stepped down from a painting, a proud, timeless Jew that transcended the fleeting history, ascending above it all in the name of his faith.

He reassured his family that the salvation from G-d comes in the blink of an eye, urging them to believe in Hashem's merciful will despite their life crashing around them. Maybe his heart was fluttering and his voice breaking, but his eyes, filled with absolute faith, instilled hope.

Shabbos waned into nightfall, and it was Sunday, dismayed and listless, replaced by Monday. Minutes crawled slowly and morbidly, in a surreal sluggish dance of a never ending torment, like when you wake up from a nightmare to yet another nightmare, as if life itself turned into a broken record, scratching the surface, churning out the same screechy notes. The city emptied out, a ghost town of abandoned houses, like a merry-go-round swirling and swirling aimlessly, with the same musical tune, though the children were long gone.

"It's time to leave," Chaim Yair decided and said to Esther. "We can't stay here any more."

They started to pack, going through the motions, just like

generations of Jews did before them, walking into the unknown, having the *Shechinah* go with them into their next exile. Somehow, Antwerp made them believe that it would never happen again, not here, not in the heart of civilized, beautiful Europe with leafy parks, ice cream stands and light rails.

Their thoughts were interrupted by a knock at the door. A tall, beautiful woman stood there, holding her young son's hand. She was Chaim Yair's cousin, a divorced woman, which was a highly unusual and frowned upon situation in those days of very traditional social norms. She was left to her own devices, having to take care of herself and her son all alone, with no family support.

Now she stood there at the door, looking lost, confused, desperate for advice, and not even sure if she would be welcomed in.

"Esther," was her first word. "What should we do?"

"We're leaving," Esther said. Brushing off all conventions, she added, "You should come with us."

Esther's words pushed this single, independent woman to make up her mind. Her decision was as final as it was paradoxical. She shook her head vigorously. "No," she said. "I'm not going anywhere."

She wasn't the only one who stayed, who didn't want to leave, to abandon their homes, to head into the unknown. Some said, "Why should we run away? So we'll go to a work camp. What's the big deal? We will do some manual labor for a while and then will go back home."

Little did anyone know what was the real, lethal meaning of the German euphemism "work camps," a conniving invention of the Nazi propaganda machine that put their potential victims at ease and in a passive state to accept their ultimate fate, and allowed opportunistic politicians across the continent and beyond who knew the real truth, to lie to their constituencies.

Little did they know that during these very days, May 14, 1940, the last Kindertransport had left, with seventy-four Jewish children whisked to safety through the neighboring Netherlands to the UK.

In Antwerp they knew nothing, and it was a fatal mistake. In that cruel new world that dawned upon Europe, unbeknownst to them, the Dark Ages had marched in. People were again to be herded and torched en masse. The Crusader crosses were replaced by swastikas and chaotic massacres were to be replaced by a well-oiled machine of industrialized extermination.

But the motivation and the zeal remained the same: to save the world from the Jews. Only the Jews didn't know history was about to repeat itself, and that they were assigned the same role in it as in the past, of ultimate imaginary villains and hence, the ultimate victims. They only found out when for many of them it was far too late.

Esther supervised the packing, but really what were they packing for? Where were they going? How long would they be gone? What kind of things would they need? Summer was about to come, so she packed only a few clothes, grabbed whatever food they had in the house, some bread, some cheese, a little chocolate, and stuffed it all in rucksacks they could easily carry.

When they left their home, they walked together to the train station, two parents and nine children. They took turns carrying Avraham Duvid, the baby. They took turns holding ten-year-old Berel who was unable to walk. His legs were swollen from rheumatoid arthritis, a degenerative autoimmune disease that deceived his body into not recognizing its own cells and attacked them as if they were the enemy. Filled with inflammation, his joints were swelling painfully, disintegrating, sapping him of weight and energy. But even his small, slight body was hard to carry for long distances.

At the cashier booth, Chaim Yair purchased tickets for his large family, and they boarded the train. Only later did they find out that they could have taken the train for free and saved the little money they had and so sorely needed. As is customary in situations of national emergency, the Belgian government nationalized the train network in an attempt to get the citizens out of harm's way, away from the onslaught of the enemy army. The trains were headed to France, but the refugees didn't know or didn't care. They only knew that they were sitting on a train with too little food, heading to nowhere, ushered away from the bombs that were falling from the sky and devouring the beautiful city they had fondly called home.

CHAPTER TWO

# The Runaways

They had plenty of time on that train: time to think, to talk to other passengers, to put together the fragmented story that slowly unraveled into something so horrifying, so crystal clear, so unflinchingly brutal in retrospect.

A story called, "the Final Solution," as if they, the Weinstein family of nine children, one of them disabled, were the problem, the existential threat to the very survival of the German nation. In Hitler's dystopian vision, Jews were the degenerative disease of mankind, just like Berel's rheumatoid arthritis, maliciously eating away at the body of the Western civilization. They had to be destroyed, utterly crushed and excised from this continent and elsewhere – from the entire world. Their collective death was deemed to pave the path to salvation of humanity, no less. And Germans were known for their methodical efficiency.

Chaim Yair shifted in his seat, tried to get comfortable, but couldn't escape the clatter of the wheels underneath him, a rhythm that bore into his bones like a throbbing scream, like a clenched fist tucked under his ribs.

When had it all started? It was a war that began only a little over a year ago, but the inevitability of it all had started years before, as early as the 1930s, when Hitler started demanding that other countries fall in line and give up land to Germany. It was not a question of "if" there will be another war, but of "when."

But as always, people preferred to live in the current moment, to savor the serenity of the fleeting now, to look away and wish away the impending catastrophe of epic proportions that was growing by the day. Europe wanted to avoid war at all costs, and there were more than enough politicians feasting on that complacency. The memories of the Great War, later to be renamed as merely "World War I," were still fresh, and though, as cruel and terrible as it was, it turned out to be only a prelude, paling in comparison with what was about to come.

Hundreds of thousands had suffered from the devastating effects of the poisonous gas used in battlefields and against the civilian population. Photos of trenches full of soldiers choking to death with mustard gas were unbearable to look at. Who knew that very soon not hundreds of thousands but millions of Jews would be gassed to death in concentration camps all across Europe.

Did the first hint come when the Belgian government started handing out gas masks that turned the wearer into what looked like a space alien? Chaim Yair didn't notice that his thoughts carried him into a state of a fitful, wearisome, restless sleep.

Sixteen-year-old Sarah, the oldest of the Weinstein's children, responsible beyond her years, a fireball of energy, a girl used to getting her way, felt unmoored. Short bursts of tooting whistles, the clattering windows, the hundreds of people shifting and moving, children crying, and whispers crawling from every direction, were drowning out her thoughts, her feelings, her very self. She heard the whispers about where the train was taking them. She didn't know what the future, if there was such a thing... would be. All she knew was that the train was taking her into the dark night, to a country she'd never seen, to a life she'd never imagined in her worst nightmares. She didn't know that the reality would transcend her wildest fears, as it would for millions more, a reality that would etch the darkest and most unfathomable chapter in world history as we know it.

It is human nature to believe that things will remain the way they were before, and nothing really bad is ever going to happen, until it's too late. In social psychology it's called confirmation bias. In real world history it's called "The Holocaust." This psychological hack was what was responsible for millions of Jews finding themselves trapped in Nazi Europe, instead of taking their lives elsewhere when it was still possible, from Palestine to the United States to the wide open Latin America.

Even though Hitler came to power in 1933 and he was very clear about his genocidal intentions toward the Jews, the war didn't start for another six more years. This would have given the Jews plenty of time to pack up and leave. But many had a very hard time recognizing what was ahead. Even the heads of European states did nothing and preferred to look away. Many wanted to simply go about their lives as if nothing ominous was about to happen.

Some attempted to bargain with Hitler or sign agreements with him, like the British Prime-Minister Chamberlain. He signed the Munich Accord, dubbed, ironically, as "Peace for Generations," which garnered him an astonishing 73% of popular support upon his return home. But then he was outsmarted by that evil, evil genius, that short mustached man with a screeching hysterical voice and a very long shadow that followed him everywhere.

Other countries even tried to ride out the wave by taking Germany's side and clutching away parcels of land from neighboring countries who didn't hustle quick enough to curry favors with the masters of the New Order.

It was early still, as the Weinstein's rode a train away from the war, but they'd find out soon enough that the ruefully unequipped and unprepared Belgian Army, would fight with great courage but prove to be totally incapable of standing up to militarily superior Germany. They capitulated on May 28, less than three weeks after the Germans launched Gelb Fall, the Code Yellow operation of capturing the Netherlands, Belgium and North France.

The train soon reached the French border and French policeman boarded to check identity documents. Chaim Yair and Esther leaned back in relief when their documents cleared inspection. They were both born in Czechoslovakia which was allied with France. But the

Jewish woman who helped Esther with her chores at home and took the same train as the Weinstein's, wasn't so lucky. She came from Romania, a country sharing the border with Czechoslovakia, with countless villages saddling both sides. In the impossible reality of war in Europe, Romania found itself allied with Germany, lest it risk a very real prospect of being subjected to a ruthless invasion by the militarist Nazi regime hungry for easy conquests.

She wasn't allowed to enter France.

The Romanian government knew that had it been overrun by the Germans, other European states would be looking away. Romanian authorities made a calculated move to align themselves with the Germans and this move of political wrangling spelled the death sentence for this poor Jewish woman.

Paradoxically, in the bureaucratic, aloof mind of a passport control official at the border, this Jewish refugee escaping Nazi persecution was deemed a potential Nazi ally, a suspect, an enemy, and was denied entry. She sobbed, stricken with terror, heartbroken, knowing full well that she was heading toward certain death, as she was forcibly removed from the train.

Esther's heart went out to her, she wished she could help her, but what could she do as a fleeing refugee with no rights and with nine children in tow? This was the first of a long string of moral tragedies of impossibility, of forced departures, of familiar faces dragged away, disappearing into the great conflagration of violence and death, of human souls trampled under the steel wheels of war.

The Weinstein's continued onward, propelled away from their quiet, picturesque country that was overrun by hateful people seeking revenge for their humiliating defeat twenty-five years earlier. Germans, an almost seventy million strong nation, attributed all the evils that befell Germany to a defenseless small group of people that counted slightly over half a million, barely three fourths of a percent of German population. But Germans went even further than that grotesque flight of paranoid imagination. In accordance with a millennia-long European tradition, they blamed the Jews, a minuscule population dispersed among other nations, for all the problems in the world, and as always, the salvation of the human race depended upon erasing the name of the Jewish people from under the sky.

In that historical mission that the Germans believed they were chosen to carry out, they had a carte blanche to do all they had to do, determined to destroy everyone and everything in their wake.

CHAPTER THREE

## *Remembering the Forgotten*

The train rattled along, the children's stomachs rumbling with hunger. How long could rationed bread and chocolate sustain them? Avraham Duvid cried with hunger and when the train stopped, Malka got off to buy milk from the villagers milling around on the platforms. They converged on the train station from the nearby vicinity to sell produce to trainloads of refugees passing through the town.

It took her a few minutes to locate a farmer pouring milk from a large tin can, and another moment for money to exchange hands. The hasty encounter was interrupted by the long whistle and wheels gearing up in accelerating motion. Malka ran, and at the last moment jumped aboard the closest car as the train was picking up speed. She stumbled in and out of cars, struggling to keep balance in a speeding train with a can full of milk in her hands, searching for her family.

In the great chaos of war, with millions of people rushing in every possible direction, many got lost and were never found, disappearing into the vortex of mass migration, of commotion and confusion. When the train started moving and Malka failed to show up, everyone in the Weinstein family panicked. Minutes of agony passed with the train devouring mile after mile of track. Malka was still missing.

In her heart, Esther blamed herself for letting Malka go. Maybe she didn't make it back, and it was her, Esther's, fault. She probably never boarded that train and now she was left behind, alone, in a foreign country, with no documents, a young vulnerable girl in the midst of the greatest madness of all called "war."

Malka was roaming train cars searching for her family, their entire life passing in front of her eyes, memories and thoughts flooding her head. She was nostalgic and scared at the same time. Wistfully, she wondered about this very moment of her life carrying a can of milk, surrounded by hundreds of people she didn't know, with documents left behind in her mother's purse, looking for her family. What if at this very moment the train stopped and border police boarded it to check passports again?

They might take her off the train as well and throw her into jail and then expel her back to her country of origin, to Czechoslovakia, a small country that was fed by its European neighbors to this hungry beast called Germany, a beast consumed with one genocidal intention: to kill all people like her...

As she bounced and balanced in the moving train, stumbling into total strangers, apologizing, exiting one car and precariously hopping over to the next, with rail tracks running under her, her thoughts kept running on their own tracks too.

She, her older sister Sarah and her younger sister Miriam were all born in Czechoslovakia. Her father, Chaim Yair, was born in Munkach, its official name Mukachevo, on February 15, 1899, to Moshe Aryeh and Faiga Mirel Weinstein.

In those days Mukachevo was part of the Austro-Hungarian Empire, but in 1920, after the defeat of Austro-Hungary and Germany in the Great War, it was incorporated into adjacent Czechoslovakia, which granted her father Czechoslovakian nationality. Then again, with the German annexation of the Sudeten region of Czechoslovakia in 1938, the pro-Nazi Hungarian government, which aided Germany in its military campaign against Yugoslavia, was granted permission by Germany to "restore its historical right" for this parcel of land in Slovakia, which it promptly acted upon on November 2, 1940.

After the end of World War II, in 1945, Mukachevo would be annexed by the Soviet Union and added to Ukraine. Her father's birthplace switched hands every twenty years or so and its real affiliation was never an established fact. Jews would be respectively called Slovak, Hungarian, Romanian, Ukrainian or Polish, but in reality these were brothers and sisters and cousins, with international borders and garrisons and artillery cutting families in half, so that sometimes first degree relatives would find themselves on two warring sides of a war.

Yet Chaim Yair Weinstein was lucky enough to be granted a Czechoslovakian nationality at the right time. Otherwise, born a subject of the Austro-Hungarian Empire, which subsequently became part of the Nazi Axis, he too, could've been taken off that train.

Her mother Esther was born in Uher-Žipov, Czechoslovakia, merely seventy miles west of Mukachevo, on February 8, 1900, shortly before Purim, and grew up in nearby Sečovce, with four siblings, three sisters and a brother. Esther's parents, Roiza and Alexander Dov Pearlman, were devout Munkacher chassidim.

Malka's parents married in 1921, a 23-year-old young man and his wife a year his junior. Immediately after their wedding, they were thrust into earning a living to support the three daughters that came in quick succession. Their livelihood didn't come easy. In post-Great War Central Europe, jobs were scarce.

Chaim Yair was a learned young man, considered a wise *talmid chacham*, even at his relatively young age. But in those troubled times between the wars, threatening negative financial headwinds were blowing across the ocean and deep into the European Continent, especially ravaging the provincial regions with scarce sources of income. The economy was at a standstill, all positions were taken, and there was nothing left that would fit his capabilities or his training as a *shochet*.

"Go to Antwerp," his Rebbe, Reb Aharon of Belz, advised him. "There you can work as a *shochet*."

Leaving his wife and children at her parent's home in Sečovce, he traveled to Antwerp seeking work, as so many like him did during those times. The job he'd hoped for didn't materialize. After a year of searching for a job, any job, Chaim Yair had enough. He couldn't bear thinking that he and his wife were forced to live separate lives with no prospect of it ever being any different. He decided that it no longer made any sense for him to be struggling, separated from his family, while his wife, Esther, was alone. If life was challenging, at least they would struggle together.

In 1928, Esther and the children left Sečovce and moved in with their father in Antwerp. As if to complicate matters, very soon after, the Stock Market on Wall Street collapsed. The Great Depression hit even harder, its shockwaves rattling Europe even more.

However, contrary to common wisdom, the wheel of fortune had turned, and as the Talmud says, the family was blessed with livelihood in the merits of the woman of the house. A week after Esther and the children arrived in Antwerp, Chaim Yair found a job as the Head Mashgiach of all the butcher stores in Antwerp. This position required both his deep understanding of *halachah*, and his practical acumen as a *shochet* who knew the ins and outs of the profession.

His employer was *Kehillas Machzikei HaDas*, which was part of the Belzer community. This was the most devoutly religious Jewish community in Antwerp. His salary was fairly decent, and on top of this the government gave a subsidy for each child.

Still, they struggled. Berel suffered from rheumatoid arthritis. His medical treatment raked up high out of pocket fees, and he often needed to be hospitalized because of his high fevers. Raising nine children was never easy, especially if one of the children is chronically ill.

Esther, alone in a city, without her parents and siblings to turn to for comfort and support, never despaired to do all she could to keep the household afloat. Typical for that era, they had a large stove with a gas range on top for cooking, which allowed her to cook and prepare all the food. However, the stove temperature couldn't be regulated enough for baking, so they had to buy their bread and challahs from the local bakery.

Esther didn't only feed her husband and nine children. There were always people knocking on the door, vagrants from Czechoslovakia and Hungary, unable to make a living there and forced to go from door to door and collect handouts. These were downtrodden people in a foreign country whose families were famished. The Weinstein's didn't have much, but they extended any help they could. Never forgetting that only a blessing from Above saved them from being just like these poor souls, Esther always invited these beggars from her home country, served them a meal that most probably was the only one they had for the day, and also put a few coins in their hands.

With the little she herself had, she would even buy things she didn't really need from the door-to-door salespeople that knocked on their door, in an effort to support them. These were not the voracious hard hitting marketing professionals dressing *haute couture*, preying on others with well-rehearsed sale pitches and inflated egos. These were humble people with a desperate look in their downcast eyes, hungry and destitute, spending lives on the road, in constant peril, peddling their cheap merchandise to put a piece of bread on the table.

The oldest girls, Sarah, Malka and Miriam, were often recruited to help cook when a neighbor made a *simchah*. Even younger Leah always tried to help, a kind and sweet girl who took after her mother. Their neighbor worked as a butcher and owned a freezer, graciously storing extra food that wouldn't stay fresh in their icebox, particularly during Yom Tov.

Their first floor apartment had five rooms including the kitchen and dining room. Sleeping space was tight for eleven people, and the girls often shared one large bed. The children loved looking through the window and watching the trolleys clattering past their apartment.

The Weinstein home was filled with Torah. Chaim Yair worked hard and long hours, and learned every spare moment he had. And he was there for his children. Always. He always made time for the endless questions of children in awe of the world. He'd wake up at five in the morning, go to the *mikvah* and *daven*, have a quick breakfast and then go to work for the rest of the day, wearing his customary black hat. Shabbos was his glimpse of Gan Eden. He'd go to *shul*, drape himself in a *tallis* and *daven* at length. Then after the meal he'd come back to *shul*, wearing his *shtreimel* and learning at his leisure.

But he couldn't walk on the streets of Antwerp in a *shtreimel*.

Antwerp only looked peaceful and laid back. In reality, anti-

Semitism was rampant throughout the entire Europe, and Jews didn't feel safe. For some reason, walking down the street in a *shtreimel* was viewed as an offense to the sensibilities of the non-Jews, in the heart of Belgium, in Antwerp, as much as in Jerusalem under the rule of the British Mandate.

Abiding by the state law, the girls went to public school. Malka was a good student and enjoyed the occasional school trips to go swimming. The girls learned Flemish, the local language of Flanders in Northern Belgium, and French, which was the official language of the land and spoken across the main parts of Belgium.

It was French, the language they learned to speak fluently, that would be a lifesaver time and again in the months that followed.

At last, Malka opened the door to the next train car and saw her family. When they saw her, after the initial moment of shocked disbelief, they rejoiced that she had appeared and had not been caught and deported. Their faces lit up with relief and great joy.

They were together again, on this train, wherever it took them. Together, they had a chance. As long as no one was lost, they could hold on to a vestige of hope that the calamity would pass and they would return to their old life unscathed...

CHAPTER FOUR

# *Montesquieu: When War Is Just a Dream*

The journey took six days. It began on Tuesday with the train coming to a final stop on Sunday in a rural area in Southern France. As it turned out later, many Belgian Jews would seek safe haven in that area.

French and Belgian humanitarian relief officials greeted the refugees at the train station, distributing food and other basic necessities. Even though from a strictly *halachic* standpoint the Weinstein's could have afforded the leniency of eating food that wasn't kosher, they instead dug into their last reserves, a few bites of chocolate. The refugees were divided into small groups and brought to nearby villages where they could stay in abandoned dilapidated houses.

Southern France, just like the rest of Europe, suffered from lack of income. Many farmers were forced to leave their properties behind and seek work in the cities, mostly as factory workers or manual laborers, huddling in the modern jungle of densely built barracks erected on top of each other, with narrow streets, polluted air, no light and rampant crime. It was a far cry from the countryside where these farmers were coming from. But what choice did they have? Either subject themselves to inhumane conditions in the intestines of an industrial city, or die of starvation back home.

The Weinstein family was brought to the small scenic village of

Montesquieu and given a large shack to accommodate their family. They were given a few blankets, sheets and pillowcases and beds made out of straw. They had a functioning bakery in Montesquieu. Finally the children had bread to eat that smelled heavenly after their long journey, and tasted even better.

The Belgian government in exile gave all the refugees a small stipend, a few francs per person for the month, which was enough to purchase the very basics to subsist on. This was a very generous and humane act, motivated by pure compassion toward displaced people who had lost everything, who were clinging to their lives.

Montesquieu was warm most of the year, a blessing to the Weinstein family who were unprepared for cold weather. They didn't have adequate clothing, nor the blankets they needed or the money to buy coal to feed the fire.

Esther made the best of their shack, feeding the children as best she could, darning and mending the fabric that was getting worn out and occasionally torn, and setting traps against the ubiquitous rats.

Montesquieu was one big family. Everyone there was a cousin of their next door neighbor. The Weinstein's were not only strangers who spoke French with an unmistakable Flemish accent, they also looked distinctly different. They were the only Jews in this village. Moreover, they were a large family of eleven, an anomaly for these people who barely had two children at most. However, Montesquieu, first bewildered, accepted the Weinstein's, their only Jews, with compassion and warmth.

Unbeknownst to them, they were a tiny piece of a much bigger puzzle. The tally of Jewish lives lost in the Holocaust was staggering, and incredibly, one needs to use big statistical numbers to talk about those lives, lumping them in the tens and hundreds of thousands, which almost makes one forget that behind each number, each name, there was a human being with a G-dly soul that lived and died, almost always violently. Nevertheless, statistics allow us to see the bigger picture and appreciate the full context of the Weinstein story.

France was occupied by the Nazis for four and a half years and between 300,000 to 400,000 French people enrolled in numerous

German military organizations and fascist movements. They actively assisted in Nazi efforts to actualize the Final Solution. Nevertheless, despite all this, only fourteen percent of French Jews and twenty-four percent of the Jews that fled to France from elsewhere, perished in the Holocaust, compared to forty percent of Belgian Jews and a staggering seventy-five percent of the Jews in the Netherlands.

The higher survival rate of French Jews was not due to the resistance of French officials to Nazi policies, or lack of effort to hunt the Jews down. Actually, it was quite the opposite. Vichy France, the one that collaborated with Nazi Germany, enforced anti-Jewish laws, including expropriation of property and mass deportations, even before they were asked to do so by Berlin.

Survival of such a vast majority of Jews on French soil was despite the big politics, and due to an entirely different factor. It was due to the vast rural parts of the country where local villagers not only allowed the newcomers to seek refuge, but actively protected them against German officials and their French collaborators. An unspoken rule was laid down by all: if you hurt a Jew, you are no longer part of our community. You are an outcast. Being an outcast in vast expanses of rural France was not a bright prospect, and even the German collaborators, who were opportunists by definition, chose to turn a blind eye on the "Jewish problem."

One French intellectual in Nazi occupied Paris said in jest, which has become a damning testimony of complicity of French elites, "Long live the shameful peace." French intellectuals were all too happy to dine and wine with finesse in trendy Parisian restaurants Maxim's and La Tour d'Argent together with their German "guests." As the military commandant of Paris said, "Out of fifty French dignitaries, forty nine asked me for personal favors and only one spoke about France."

In contrast, the French villagers dug their heels deep into the mud and let these other foreigners, the unfortunate ones, the Indésirables, as they were defined by official orders, the odd looking people, the Jews, hide among them.

The unvarnished les misérables of France, the country folks, men and women that lived on their farms and homesteads in poverty stricken rural France, collectively replied to their arrogant, treacherous and morally corrupt compatriots strutting down the sidewalks of Champs de Elysee, basking in the limelight of theater stages and huddling in trendy cafes, denizens of privileged and famously indulgent higher echelons of Parisian social scene, as it were. "We will atone for this national disgrace by hiding the innocents, by closing ranks around them and refusing to turn them in."

The Weinstein's were lucky to find themselves among these simple, charitable people who in the midst of the great massacre of humanity decided to go against the politics of hustle and moral decay.

After a day or two, Chaim Yair and Esther went to Port-Sainte-Marie, a nearby community about six miles away, where a farmers' market still offered some produce. They were able to bring back provisions that lasted for a few days. But this option didn't last long. Ten days later, the Germans marched through the city and confiscated everything they found.

Toiling to find the provisions to feed their family became an ongoing ordeal. The Weinstein's bought whatever they could – milk, cheese, eggs – from homesteads and farms dotting the area.

In the small village, the newly arrived refugees fashioned a sort of life for themselves. Chaim Yair planted a small vegetable garden where he grew carrots and some greens. The children would play outside, fighting off the ever present hunger, distracting themselves from the oppressive endlessness of empty time with nothing else to do, with no school and no books.

But more than that, they were busy suppressing the fear of what tomorrow might bring, fearing every cloud of dust rising at the horizon and wondering if it was a procession of German trucks on their way to take them away to a place with no return.

Four year-old Naftoli would spend days watching the butcher next door, transfixed. It was not the fact of the animal slaughter that made Naftoli so caught up in the scene, but the inhumane way it was done. For as long as Naftoli remembered, his father worked as the *mashgiach* of all the butcher stores in Antwerp, so he grew up knowing a thing or two about *shechitah* and where the meat was coming from. Here, whatever it was that the local butcher did, it looked much more savage and unsavory than the *shechitah* that Naftoli had observed back home.

His father often sat beside him, sharpening his *chalof*, the *shechitah* knife. Chaim Yair would always carry his *chalof* with him so that if an opportunity presented itself for him to buy a chicken, a rare find in those challenging times, he wouldn't let it pass by, but instead he was ready to perform *shechitah* on the spot. In this way there was always the possibility of providing his children with a bowl of chicken soup, a piece of chicken, and a stew made from the leftovers.

Naftoli had a memory of his father, before all the madness descended upon them, when Naftoli was only a toddler, sitting at the table eating chicken. In jest his father extended his hand and pretended to grab his chicken, and then gave it back to him. In his memory, there was his father's laughing face. His father's eyes, usually filled with mystery and devotion, were softening for a moment with simple, warm, embracing love for his little boy.

Such an insignificant moment that could've been washed away in the stream of tumultuous events, somehow remained etched in Naftoli's memory, like a special moment in time, flooded in soft late afternoon light pouring through the windows, a nostalgic snapshot of the past long gone.

Decades later, this small unmemorable moment would bring Naftoli to tears, the beautiful, unassuming plainness of it, of the simple, humble life that was trampled and crushed by the manic ambition of the Hitler's of the world.

But then he was too young to know that the world around him had gone mad. He could daydream about the big luscious *hamentashen* his mother baked on Purim, and the fluffy *kneidlach* on Pesach. He tried not to complain when all he had to eat for days and weeks on end were the carrots from the little vegetable garden that his father planted in the backyard. It was still an adventure then, a holiday of sorts, like a journey into the unknown, a different world where he could play outside for hours in the warm sultry weather, or herd cows down the dirt road and into a field, that special time when a local villager handed Naftoli a stick and asked him to help him.

In a time of war, one had to learn to accept life as it was. The Weinstein's were adept at this remarkable quality, so vital in those days. The butcher's wife owned her own camera, a commodity almost as exceptional in this tiny village as a privately owned car was back in Antwerp. She snapped a memorable photo where everyone put on a beautiful smile, as if caught casually in the middle of a leisurely family vacation, with their eyes squinted against the shining sun.

Here was Malka, to her mother's right, with an assertive, open face and beautiful hair, lighting up the photo with the warm smile of an eldest daughter who knows how to care for her younger siblings, to share the responsibilities of running a big family, and never fails to appreciate the joys of life. And then there is Sarah, to the left of her father, who seems a bit shy, but content, snuggled in the midst of this close-knit family. Then there is Miriam with an unabashedly broad smile that fully displays her brilliant personality of a happy warrior, who leans in, ready to pick up a conversation, to extend a helping hand, to be there for whoever needs her, never conceding defeat at the hands of any unkind circumstance that might befall her. And she will remain just like that for the rest of her life, unbroken by any adversity she has to face.

Even in this fleeting moment captured by an amateur photographer friend, Miriam is doing what she always did, supporting her brother Berel who suffered from rheumatoid arthritis and could barely stand on his feet.

The smaller children are in the bottom row: Avraham Duvid, Gittele, Yankel, Leah and Naftoli, with the boys sporting berets and the girls wearing ribbons, a staple accessory of a typical French village child, all smiling and laughing towards the camera. Yes, this is a photo of a happy family on an outing to the countryside.

Only Chaim Yair and Esther, their parents, look like a great burden weighs them down, an existential angst hiding at the corners of their mouths, lurking in their sunken eyes. They are responsible for the daily survival of their family, always sensing the unstoppable prowling of the Nazi monster behind their backs, feeling the chill of the long, dark shadow that threatens to overwhelm them all at any moment, without knowing when that moment will come...

CHAPTER FIVE

# Gurs: The First Rung of Purgatory

AUGUST 1940

After the Germans crushed the Allies in the Low Countries, the Netherlands and Belgium, they simply took a detour and bypassed the celebrated and exorbitantly costly Maginot Line – a state of the art line of fortifications impervious to most forms of attack that the French spent a decade to erect – and broke into France through the Ardennes Forest and across the River Meuse. The Allied Forces found themselves encircled by the Germans, with their backs to the Atlantic, and scrambled to retreat across the English Channel, barraged by German constant fire. That hasty rescue of tens of thousands of Allied servicemen to the British Islands came to be known in military history as *The Miracle at Dunkirk*, which lasted eight days and nights, from May 26 to June 4, 1940. As lucky as it may have been to the embattled British and French troops that escaped the Continent, mostly intact, it left France defenseless in the face of German rapid advance. Sure enough, the Germans took over the entire France, roughly twice the size of Germany, within six short weeks after the Fall of Gelb had begun.

Germany and France signed the Armistice of 22 June, 1940, establishing a German occupation zone in Northern and Western France, leaving the Southeast France "free" to be governed by the French. The French government evacuated to Vichy in southern France, and was called Vichy France. Free in name only, it wasn't long before Vichy

France became a client state headed by a puppet government that obediently did the Germans bidding. Tragically, no other than the French war hero Philippe Petain, an 84-year-old retired commander-in-chief hailed as the Marshal of France, rendered respectability to Vichy France by becoming its Prime Minister. He was known as "the Victor of Verdun" after the greatest war achievement of France during the Great War that was attributed to this simple man who rose in ranks due to his genuine ability and valor. He exemplified everything France was proud of, but also became the most manifest example of the mockery France had become. Germans manipulated this elderly man who was hopelessly out of his depth, suffering from the cognitive frailty that came with his age.

It must have been a very special form of entertainment for the German officials to humiliate Petain by feeding his fantasy of being no other but a modern Joan of Arc, saving France.

In June 1940, Vichy France circulated a postcard with aging Petain's photograph and a patriotically inspired inscription, "I have been with you in the glorious days, I am with you in the dark days, be by my side." He, now turned into a pitiful man, the very embodiment of moral capitulation mixed with personal hubris, took France to its darkest days ever imagined.

Thus France, swiftly and humiliatingly defeated, did all it could to telegraph "business as usual" under the occupation regime. Ordinary people got the message and went about their daily business, making survival their main goal. The refugees started trickling back home.

The battle of Belgium was lost, France was crushed, the fighting was over, and the time had come to return home, was what the Belgians and the French concluded. The Germans let them be, and French folks went along. It was not their war after all, they reckoned. Common sense said that in the Great War the French humiliated the Germans, now Germans slapped the French on the wrist, and now let's go back to making it work between neighbors. War was kind of an anomaly, a rematch of a previous time around, and everyone was more than happy to call it quits. German soldiers and officers loved Paris, and Paris showered its charm on them in response. Not a single German in uniform was hurt in Paris during the first year and a half of occupation. It was as though everyone was declaring, "Let's go back to regular life, as if nothing happened!"

Only the Weinstein's, like thousands of other Jewish families, uprooted and scrambling to survive, had nowhere to go back to. The vast south of France still conveyed a sense of comparative safety, with Jews scattered across forgotten poor villages among a population that minded their own business and secretly loathed the crass Germans. They were much safer there than they'd be in Antwerp under the direct rule of the Germans. Here in southern France, they didn't have to wear a Jewish star and could still travel.

But it wouldn't last forever.

※

They were sitting in the garden, Chaim Yair and Esther, enjoying a rare moment of quiet. No news was good news.

They weren't expecting the French policemen who appeared out of nowhere, asking for Chaim Yair's papers. "What's your name?" one of them asked. "Where are you from?"

The policemen gave his papers a cursory glance, barely listening to his responses. They must have known of the Weinstein's from the first day of their arrival. They clearly stood out as foreigners, of a very specific creed. But until now they didn't bother to do anything about it. The times had changed overnight, and individuals like Chaim Yair Weinstein had to disappear from the pages of history.

Opportunistic, caring for their own livelihood, these two French policemen were dutifully doing the German bidding. If you'd come to them thirty years later and ask, "Why did you take this man who did nothing wrong, to his almost certain death?" – They'd probably answer what their superiors answered a few years later when tried at Nuremberg for war crimes against humanity. They'd shrug and say, "We carried out orders."

Evil was now an everyday norm. They smiled politely and went about their daily duties, to dispatch another package to its destination. They marched Chaim Yair away.

Even if you lie in bed during long sleepless nights, when your worst fears knock on the door, that dreadful moment still leaves you shell-shocked and lost. The Weinstein's, stunned, unable to move, to utter a word, watched their father walk away, flanked by two quintessentially well-mannered French policemen, as if a trapdoor with a fiery volcano threatening to consume them, had flung open under their feet.

When a tragedy strikes, often the biggest shock is the sense that this is a moment of no return, that life as you knew it will never be the same, and you can do nothing to turn the time back. The inevitability of time flowing in only one direction is the scariest feeling of it all. You can't erase that dreadful picture of a man you love and trust, and your very existence depends on him, walking away and disappearing into the unknown, with his hands tied behind his back. You can't forget it. Worse still, you can't undo it. We don't yet have a mechanism to rewind time.

It was like on Tisha B'Av, Malka thought to herself, like the destruction of a Temple, of a family. A life interrupted.

Chaim Yair was taken to Gurs internment camp, merely ninety miles southwest of Montesquieu. Just like Auschwitz in Southern Poland, which was an anonymous, mostly abandoned assortment of one-story wrecked shacks and dilapidated barracks left behind by Austrian and Polish armies and by transient workers, and haphazardly renovated in May, 1940, to become a makeshift detention center for Polish political prisoners, the Gurs Internment Camp in southwest France was also merely an afterthought. It was a defunct compound of unlivable shacks hastily used for an influx of a new kind of prisoner population. Located in proximity to the French-Spanish border, originally it was set up in 1939 by the French government for refugees fleeing the Spanish Civil War.

Same as in Auschwitz, Gurs would later be reused as a detention site for the Jews that would be transported there. However, unlike its infamous "big brother," it never grew in size and sophistication to become an industrial machine of mass murder. Compared to Auschwitz, Majdanek, Treblinka, and other massive concentration camps about to be built within the next few years, Gurs remained a boutique establishment of sorts, where no mass executions were ever carried out.

Nevertheless, Gurs holds a dark historical record in its own right, as a harbinger of the moral mutilation of Europe that was later to come. Gurs was the first place ever designated as a deportation destination where the Jews would be concentrated to await their later fate. Two long years would pass before the Wannsee Conference would take place in January 1942, where the Final Solution of the Jewish Question – that strategic operational plan of the Nazi Germany to perpetrate genocide of the Jewish people – would be adopted.

First signs of an impending catastrophe were already showing, even though no one seemed able to envision the epic proportions of evil that were about to happen.

On October 3, 1940 the Statute on the Jews was issued, and three weeks later the Wagner-Burckel Aktion was carried out: 7,500 Jews from the Baden and Alsace-Lorraine regions in southwestern part of Germany were rounded up, loaded on seven trains that headed southwest, and deported across border, to a newly conquered France.

In orderly Germany, the entire operation took place "without friction or incident" and was "scarcely noticed by the population," as the Nazis boasted. The concept proved it, the deportation went mostly unnoticed, and general public went about their business, perhaps slightly unnerved by what they glimpsed, or maybe relieved that their nosy and noisy Jewish neighbors vanished at once. As the Nazi official overseeing the operation succinctly put it, Baden and Alsace were the first part of Germany to become Judenrein, "clean of Jews." He was proud of his achievement.

Most of the deportees found themselves locked up by the Vichy government at Gurs Internment Camp.

Using the same Statute on the Jews as a legal framework, Vichy French authorities detained as many Jews across France as they could find, including Chaim Yair Weinstein. Gurs was the destination where the Jews accounted for the majority of its entire detainee population, eighteen thousand out of the total of twenty-two thousand.

Three years after the first Jew entered the gates of Gurs Camp and nine months after the Final Solution became the supreme law of the land, almost four thousand of the Jewish prisoners of Gurs were transferred in six convoys to Drancy Deportation Camp, a building complex in a northeastern suburb of Paris initially used for prisoners of war. Originally constructed as a residential complex, the horseshoe-shaped construction was converted into a police barracks. With the arrest of several thousand Jewish men in Paris in August 1941, Drancy gradually would become one of the central assembly camps where tens of thousands of Jews from France would pass through. Beginning in the summer of 1942, the detainees were systematically taken to extermination camps in Poland, Auschwitz being their primary destination.

The life of misery and the daily struggle for survival struggle continued.

Gurs Internment Camp was a small strip of land less than a mile long and six hundred and fifty feet wide, enclosed in a double barbed wire fence, creating a no man's corridor on the perimeter where the guards were patrolling the camp, with one long street spanning the length of it. The entire territory of the camp was divided into small parcels of land, called "islets," 300 x 600 feet each, separated one from the other by an enclosure of barbed wire. Six of those islets, or blocks, lined up one side of the street and seven more lined up on the other. Each islet comprised of thirty or so cabins, with a total of three hundred and eighty-two of them. Made of thin planks of wood, covered by tarred fabric for a roof, and measuring a meager two hundred and seventy square feet, these cabins lodged up to sixty inmates in each one. With no windows or insulation, originally designed during the Great War as a temporary structure for soldiers arriving to a frontline and awaiting their trench assignment, they didn't offer protection from cold and the elements, and rapidly deteriorated under the torrential rains so common in Gurs due to its proximity to the Atlantic Ocean.

Because of poor drainage, the grounds of the camp were basically a year round knee deep puddle of muddy clay. In vain attempt to not drown in it, the inmates made paths with the few stones they could scavenge. They stripped pieces of wire and stretched them between the cabins and the toilets, like the railing of a staircase, to maintain balance under the wind and the rain on slippery, treacherous ground.

Outhouses were open wooden platforms, six feet high and with no walls or roofs, placed between the cabins, with massive tubs underneath to collect the waste. When they'd overflow, the waste would be transported off the grounds in carts. Due to poor sanitary conditions and putrid, humid environment, infectious diseases were rampant. During the first two years, dysentery and typhus claimed the lives of eight hundred detainees, about four percent of the entire detainee population.

As harsh as the conditions were, this place was not designated to torture or kill people. Its rudimentary fences and lack of lookout towers manned by machine guns, made it more possible to escape. If one could pass for a local and had a bit of cash sewed into his clothes, he could find a tear in the fence and take a daring dash for freedom. But anyone who looked different or didn't speak the local dialect didn't stand a chance. He'd be captured and returned.

However, unlike other places, the punishment for attempted escape would not necessarily be an on the spot execution, but rather solitary confinement. Only repeat offenders would be shipped off to other camps where they'd most probably meet their death.

Comparative ease of escape and absence of capital punishment for the first failed attempts prompted seven hundred and fifty-five successful escapes during the three year existence of the Gurs Internment Camp. However, Chaim Yair, a foreigner whose appearance and accent would betray instantly, didn't even attempt to run away.

Until he did.

---

For three weeks Chaim Yair's family cried over the disappearance of their father, with no idea if they would ever see him again. But then life had to go on. They had learned to leave home behind, and now, in the middle of Holocaust, they had to even learn to leave loved ones behind.

One day a sign appeared that all children must report to the City Hall to get vaccinated. Like everything else in their lives, medical authorities were extremely authoritarian and public health was very strictly enforced. It was not an issue of "good will" or "informed medical decision." That traditional society, with its rigid chain of authority, dictated that there was no room left for dissent of opinion. Missing the vaccination would be an unthinkable infraction of rules of conduct in those conformist days.

They had to sit quietly on a long wooden bench with their hands folded neatly in their lap and patiently wait for their shot. "Children should be seen, not heard," an old adage goes, especially while waiting in a line for a nurse in a starched white apron and a snow white cap with a red cross in front.

If there was a sign, all complied, not even thinking twice.

Esther sent Malka there with the younger children.

Malka was sitting in the hallway of the City Hall, waiting for their names to be called, when a neighbor came over and sat next to her.

"You know," she said casually, "your father is home."

Malka just stared at her, not letting her heart believe her ears.

"How do you know?" she hardly dared to ask. "I just saw him," the woman replied. "Go and see with your own eyes."

"Can...can you watch my siblings for a few minutes?" Malka pleaded. Taking them with her and missing their vaccination was certainly not an option, even if her father had apparently risen from the dead.

"Yes, I will watch them. Go, go!"

Malka ran, heart thumping in her chest, the short distance between their home and the City Hall. Could it be true?

Within minutes Malka was running up to the big garden in front of their house. Even before she saw him, Malka heard her father's voice from inside the house. As her heart had refused to believe it was happening when he was escorted away, now her heart struggled again to accept his miraculous return.

She stood at the door, looking in at him and felt as if she was in a dream, viewing herself from the outside. Affection – modest, shy, at times lacking expressivity, ran deep in their family. Leaning against the doorpost, Malka could feel the love and joy mixed with disbelief at his great fortune pouring out of her father and across the room, as if he was seeing his family for the first time in his life.

He had quite a story to tell. It was a desperate decision made in a flash of a moment, as he was led away. At that split second he made a choice so many tragically didn't make, not to surrender to the fate forced upon him by a faceless bureaucracy of genocide. Knowing the bloody heritage of Jewish history in Europe, Chaim Yair had a foreboding feeling that he shouldn't surrender his fate to others. He chose to run, risking instant death from a bullet in his back instead of a slow, torturous death of a decaying remainder of a human being corralled in one of the barracks of a slaughterhouse called Europe under the Nazis.

After a few uneventfully long and dreadfully harsh weeks in Gurs, marked with the daily struggle for survival in a confined inhospitable space with nothing to do, Chaim Yair was summoned to travel with two armed guards to a different location. Where or what the purpose was, he had no idea, but wherever it was, he knew it wouldn't be good.

As inhumanely difficult as the living conditions in Gurs were, the authorities there weren't handed down an order to actually make people die, and didn't show the inclination to do so on their own accord. They may have been complicit of collaboration but they didn't rush to get their hands dirty. For this purpose, whatever the cause, the inmates would be dispatched to a different camp. Chaim Yair knew that a transition meant only one thing. Because of a missing stamp on some anonymous paper, or a mixed up number, or some other inexplicable technicality, he was sentenced to die. The banality of annihilation was astounding.

The guards marched him to a train station. They meant no evil, nor were they on high alert. They were just doing their job, escorting him to his next destination, and he was expected to do his job, to disappear with no protesting. The two guards stood there, on an empty strip of concrete, a platform of a remote train station. They knew all too well that the Jew they brought had nowhere to go. Two solitary tracks flanked the platform, surrounded by forests.

A long whistle signaled a train approaching the station, heading in an opposite direction. Chaim Yair waited until a moment before the train doors closed shut, and took a running leap into the train compartment. The doors slammed behind him, and the train started accelerating, scurrying him away, leaving the stunned guards on the platform.

The station didn't have a superintendent to pull the emergency stop, nor did the guards make much of an effort to signal for the train to stop. And so, there he was making his way back to his family!

In a chaos of war that accounted for staggering statistics, estimating seventy to eighty million people participating in combat on all sides, with fifty to sixty million military and civilian casualties, nine billion pounds of explosives used, hundreds of millions of displaced people frantically fleeing in every direction, improbable things were happening, mostly devastating, but some of them quite miraculous.

Chaim Yair's escape was one of those miracles, barely noticeable in the great upheaval. But it was a story of one human being with a beating heart and G-dly soul, leaping to life, even if short lived.

Esther's heart had broken in pieces when her Chaim Yair was taken away. Now, when he returned, the shards of her heart started to knit together, but something inside her remained shattered and wouldn't heal.

Was it the sense of vulnerability that hit her and never let up? Was it the thoughts of how illusory the quiet days could be, when the lurking danger is slowly, inevitably creeping up? Was it the excruciating pain of thinking that the person she was so attached to for so many years was suffering somewhere out in the big, dangerous world, and she couldn't be there with him? Whatever the precise cause was, the effort to keep the family together in her husband's absence, had worn her down. She had a hard time keeping up with everything and everyone, and gradually more and more responsibility shifted to her older daughters, Sarah, Malka and Miriam.

They genuinely cared for their mother, and knew that it was not just about them. Sometimes a person, as resilient and resourceful as they may be, crosses that invisible line where others have to take over. This is what families are for. Without needing to say a word, Esther's daughters knew one simple fact: they were called to step in and do what they had to do.

And they did.

CHAPTER SIX

# *Aix Les Bains: The Beauty and the Beast*

SEPTEMBER–NOVEMBER 1940

It was too dangerous for Chaim Yair and his family to stay any longer in the small village that had sheltered them. Not only the Weinstein's but the villagers as well would face reprisals if the authorities found him there, a fugitive that no one cared to turn in. If they didn't pick up and dissolve into the night, it would be only a question of time, a day, maybe just a few hours, before the entire village, tolerant of their presence so far, would turn on them, or put them all in the line of fire. The Weinstein's had to leave before their door would be broken down.

Many Jewish families that fled from Antwerp converged on the other end of the country, three hundred and fifty miles away, in Aix Les Bains. This was a beautiful resort near the Franco-Swiss border renowned since Roman antiquity for its hot springs. Moving there would serve a dual purpose. First and foremost, they'd slip away from their last known address and hope for their tracks to be lost in the turmoil of war and mass displacement. But also, Aix-Les-Bains could be beneficial for Berel. Berel still couldn't walk, his joints painfully inflamed, and the baths of Aix Les Bains were known to soothe and even heal arthritis.

Although Chaim Yair hoped and prayed for a cure, he couldn't forget the day he brought Berel to get a *brochah* from the Belzer Rebbe.

Chaim Yair traveled with his son two hundred miles across the border, to Belz, a small town forty miles north of Lemberg in eastern Poland (today Western Ukraine) where one of the greatest *Chassidic* Masters, Rabbi Aharon Rokeach, lived.

Rabbi Aharon Rokeach was known among Jews and non-Jews alike as the "Wonder Rebbe." He was truly a wondrous man, of great power of prayer and of exceptional spiritual insight. But he earned his nickname for a much more tangible reason, for the wonders he performed on a regular basis. He was a man who lived in a different dimension, and spiritual realms were transparent to him.

Their son Berel's full name was Yissochor Dov, after the Belzer Rebbe's father and predecessor. Chaim Yair traveled to the Rebbe with the special hope that the Rebbe would have special compassion for a disabled boy who bore his illustrious father's name. Chaim Yair hoped that the Rebbe would be able to see into Berel's soul and repair what needed to be repaired, and restore his frail body to full health.

At the audience the Rebbe granted him, Chaim Yair first asked for permission to leave his job as *mashgiach*. He had a small grocery store that he could eke out a living from, if need be. Chaim Yair was scrupulously strict when it came to *halachah*, and the butcher establishments in Antwerp resented his "meddling" in their businesses as a supervisor of their *kashrus*. He grew tired of continuous altercations with them, and pleaded with the Rebbe to grant him permission to leave the job.

"No," the Rebbe said. "You must continue your work." Chaim Yair then turned to his son Berel. "Please give him a *brachah* for a full recovery," he said, adding, "His name is Yissachar Dov."

"He will be a good Jew," the Rebbe answered.

With his sharp instincts, Chaim Yair heard not only what the Rebbe said, but more importantly, what he refused to say. "Please," Chaim Yair begged. "A *brachah* for health."

"He will be an honest Jew," the Rebbe added, unmoved in his resolve not to say what Chaim Yair so desperately wanted him to say. A *Tzaddik* ordains and G-d makes it true, as the Talmud says numerous times. But this time the *Tzaddik* remained silent, and Chaim Yair knew the bitter truth, his son would not recover.

Berel's soul descended to this world to suffer these afflictions all the days he was allotted to be here. But the Rebbe promised – and it came to be true – stunted growth wouldn't make the light of Berel's soul any dimmer. During his life, Berel's outsized personality, deep intelligence, sharp sense of humor and a talent at striking up friendships, would make people overlook his deformed physique. The pain though, wouldn't let Berel forget his ailment for a second.

Even if it only offered temporary relief, the hot springs of Les Bains were worth the journey. A curious, quite improbable and mostly forgotten piece of World War II history is that many Jews converged on Les Bains during the first phase of the war. As part of an Axis, the Italian Army waged a brief and largely unsuccessful Battle of the Alps. France succeeded in defending the Alps and never surrendered the mountainous range to the Italians. Due to its defeat to Germany on other fronts, France was forced to sign an armistice with Italy, a German ally. That armistice came into effect on the same date as the armistice with Germany. Under this armistice, signed in Rome, Italy demanded comparatively modest concessions. Italian ambitions lay elsewhere, not so much on the Continent but in the Mediterranean Basin, including French colonies in North Africa.

As far as French territory went, Italy occupied only a comparatively minor patch of land in the southeastern part of France, where it established a demilitarized zone and reserved the right to interfere as far west as Auvergne-Rhône-Alpes region, including the department of Savoie where Aix-Les-Bains was located.

Thus, while technically under the French, Aix-Les-Bains found itself under the Italian military rule, which led to one of those incalculable paradoxes that human history is replete with. When under the Statute on the Jews in late 1940, the French Prefecture started carrying out a campaign of arrests of indésirables, Jews of foreign origin who came from outside of France. The Italian Occupation Forces asserted their prerogative to secure the Jews from any deportations.

Even as late as 1942, Italian brigadier general Avarna di Gualtieri, representing the Italian High Command in Vichy, wrote a curt letter to Admiral Platon, in which he demanded release of eight Jews arrested in Annecy. He went further and demanded that no Jews whatsoever, of any nationality, be they French, Italian, Swiss or from any other country, would fall under the French jurisdiction, but rather be directly overseen by Italian authorities.

History books attribute Italian aggressive interference with French policies mostly to a historical rivalry between the two countries dating hundreds of years back. This antagonism, so the history textbook logic goes, caused Italians to contradict the French even when they were carrying out a policy that Italians should have been supportive of, specifically that concerning repression of the Jews. This narrative, however, ignores the fact that Mussolini, as controversial a figure as he was in a broader political context, pointedly refused to allow the Final Solution to be carried out on Italian territory and denied Hitler the opportunity to persecute Italian Jews until the very last minute. Shielding Jews from prosecution went even as far as Italian diplomats carrying out concerted efforts to provide Jews with travel documents that would allow them to escape Nazi persecution.

Just one example of many is that of Dino Alfieri, an Italian Ambassador in Berlin in 1940–1942. In 1940, Alfieri sent a proposal to the Italian foreign ministry to protect the rights of Italian Jewish citizens residing in France. The Italian Foreign Ministry approved Alfieri's request to protect citizenship and property rights of French Jews.

On September 2, 1942, Ambassador Alfieri was successful in his formal request that the German Foreign Office delay the application of anti-Semitic racial laws in North Africa. Further, he persuaded the German high command in Tunisia not to take measures against Jews of Italian nationality without the consent of the Italian Consul General there. Over five thousand Italian Jews in Tunisia were thus left unharmed. An interesting detail of this story is that this diplomatic effort was executed with direct approval of the Foreign Ministry of Italy.

Likewise, Giuseppe Bastianini, Italian Governor of Dalmatia (an historical heartland of Croatia), in 1941–43, was directly involved in protecting Jewish refugees in the Italian zone of occupation from deportation and murder. When, in February 1943, he proceeded to be appointed the Undersecretary of the Italian Foreign Ministry, Giuseppe Bastiannini submitted a memorandum for the signature of Mussolini to protect Jews in the Italian zones of occupation. He argued that the Italian Army and diplomatic corps must not collaborate in the killing of Jews.

On two separate occasions, he told Mussolini that if he signed an order for deportation of Jews, the responsibility for their deaths would be his.

Some say that Mussolini refused to let the Germans carry out their genocidal policies in the territories due to personal ambitions, to show his people that he was an independent leader and not a puppet of the Germans. However, it was too far reaching of a policy to depend solely on personal hubris. It would be a consistent official position of the Italian government pushing back against the genocidal policies of the Germans.

In 1942, the Italian military commander in Croatia refused to hand over Jews in his zone to the Nazis. In January, 1943, the Italians refused to cooperate with the Nazis in rounding up the Jews living in the occupied zone of France under their control and in March they prevented the Nazis from deporting Jews in their zone. German Foreign Minister Joachim von Ribbentrop even conveyed a veiled threat, complaining that "Italian military circles...lack a proper understanding of the Jewish question."

This is one of countless examples of how paradoxical history can get.

Besides the Jewish lives spared by the Italian occupation forces in Italian controlled parts of France, in Italy proper the Jews fared even better, if such a word can be used speaking about the Holocaust and lost human lives. However, the cold numbers tell their story. Out of 44,500 Italian Jews, 7,682 would perish in Holocaust, which amounts to 17% of Jewish population of Italy. None of them died at the hands of Italians, but directly at the hands of the Germans, after Italy was overrun by the German army in 1943. This speaks to a collective conscience of Italians as a nation.

Fascist Italy, member of an Axis, a military ally of Nazi Germany, was actively shielding Jews from annihilation, extending its authority over a country that officially is viewed by historians as a part of an Allied force, albeit under occupation. Those designated as "bad" actively rescued Jews from the hands of those inscribed in the historical books as "good." Go figure the controversies of human history, which do not fit neatly into simple formulae of "good versus evil," or "Allies vs. Axis."

Italians, as ashamed as they are to this day of having been forced to choose the wrong side of history in the middle of the twentieth century, tried as best they could to not cross the line of moral depravity, unlike the Poles and the Ukrainians who are judged leniently by historians as the "victims" of German invasion, while in reality they took an active and sinister role in carrying out the evil, and willingly participated in the mass extermination of the Jews who had lived alongside them for over nine hundred years...

Chaim Yair and his daughter Malka went on a scouting trip to Aix-Les-Bains to find accommodations and prepare the way for their family to move there. Of course they noticed that Aix-Les-Bains was a stunning resort town hugging the slope of Mont Revard, an auxiliary of Bauges Mountain range, that ran down to a large lake, Luc du Bourget. There were stately manors and palaces that occupied the high parts of town, with lush parks and wide boulevards lined by old trees, cafes overflowing to sidewalks, and a large marina in the lower part of the town, docked by rocking boats with tied sails. Forests, mirrored in the pristine water, stretched up the mountains on the other side of the lake.

Aix-Les-Bains was a haven for the high heeled and the successful. In the midst of all this serenity, one could barely feel the war raging around Europe.

And in the midst of this spectacular place hid a whole different kind of crowd: the *indésirables*, the Jewish refugees that were hunted down all across France. Here, under Italian military rule, they were comparatively secure, not harassed by French Prefecture, until further notice. Many of them came from Antwerp, where just a couple years earlier, when they lived in peace and prosperity, they were vacationing as desirable guests with deep pockets.

*Who could imagine,* Malka was thinking, *that just a few years would pass and they'd revisit this picturesque town as migrants fleeing persecution, fighting for survival.*

*We don't need something fancy,* Malka thought to herself. *We only need a place to rest our heads.*

In *shul,* Chaim Yair met former neighbors who explained to him the logistics: where to rent a house, who were the "good guys" to talk to and who were the "bad guys" to scrupulously avoid.

Scouting trip successful, it wasn't long before they found a house that was large enough to accommodate their family. The house boasted a full kitchen with metal pots and pans that would not be so complicated to *kasher* in a container of boiling water.

Chaim Yair found a *shochet* he knew, a refugee from Germany who fled to Antwerp at the beginning of the war. Chaim Yair only trusted the *kashrus* standards of a few of the *shochets* in Antwerp, and fortunately, this *shochet* happened to be one of them.

Now they had kosher meat, but their house wasn't *kashered* yet, nor did they have all the other ingredients to make this slice of raw meat into a full meal. They searched for and finally found a woman who agreed to prepare it for them in her *kosher* kitchen.

As much as Malka happily anticipated tasting meat again, after so much time had passed that they hadn't had any, she was greatly disappointed when she actually tasted it. The woman simply boiled the meat in a pot filled with water, without making any effort to add spices or a couple of potatoes or even a slice of onion, to offer a real meal for the starved father and daughter who had traveled from afar.

An inconsequential thing, Malka knew that. She knew that being alive was already huge, having her father miraculously return and their entire family alive and together, was more than one could hope for in their wildest dreams. It wasn't about food. It was about human care, about making this world a place where people genuinely expressed concern for one another.

Those shocking, jarring moments when she'd see someone lacking compassion, would sting forever. She couldn't help but think of her mother who would welcome every visitor, every vagrant, every pauper knocking on her door, with so much kindness and love. Her mother would have done all she could to turn that piece of meat into a tasty labor of love, knowing how precious it was for its downtrodden owner to experience not only the energy gained from the needed nutrition, but the special ingredient of love and nurturing that the person eating it would know that they were not only provided with food to carry on for another day, but that somebody genuinely cared, that they were not alone in a wide world reeking of loneliness and despair.

That barely noticeable fleeting moment in her youth, of eating a chunk of bland meat cooked by a strange woman who didn't care enough, turned into a formative event, a lesson she learned for life. Though she tried to judge this woman favorably, she realized that people were different indeed, and the world was the way it was not because of some external circumstances or random events. But because every single moment, every smile, every kind word and deed, made all the difference whether the world was wonderful or less so. Not everyone loved everyone like her mother did, Malka knew now.

Maybe the tension of all that had happened was overwhelming her with these negative thoughts about the kind woman who was willing to cook the meat at all, but at that moment, the light seeping through the window seemed slightly dimmer on that late afternoon.

The rest of the family joined them in Aix-Les-Bains. The garden apartment was beautiful, a full floor of large rooms and wide windows, filled with air and light. Their landlady was an elderly woman who was always wearing black clothes, and lived upstairs with her niece.

As time went by and they were settled in, Malka ventured up to their apartment every now and then to use their landlady's sewing machine, to mend or do alterations on her siblings' clothes. The niece would sit next to Malka and chat, and time would fly by pleasantly. She shared stories about her aunt's austere ways, of the three potatoes being cooked every single day for lunch, even though the widow was not in dire financial need and could afford better food.

Though she was once married, it was only for a very brief time. Then her husband was killed in the Great War. She had never remarried and didn't have any children. That was why her niece, who wasn't married, lived with her.

Mourning her loss had become a lifestyle, wearing black clothes for the last nearly thirty years. Her ascetic upbringing exacerbated her ongoing grief as a faithful widow, compelling her to save every penny, to stick to a rigid, exacting, joyless life as a spinster.

When she would venture out to the street, her expressionless face, skin and bones thin body draped in black, she stood out in stark contrast to the festive, lively colors of their resort town.

During the period that the Weinstein family stayed in Aix-Les-Bains, Berel was able to spend time immersed in the natural hot springs every day. Slowly, he showed some improvement. At the start of the war, Berel had to be carried everywhere. After that healing time that he spent in the hot springs, he could limp on his own.

Relationships between the Catholic Church and the Jews were never simple, with a past marred by massacres all across Europe at the hands of crusaders, incited by the church. Nevertheless, the very first Friday they were in Aix-Les-Bains, the local Catholic priest, a friendly young man fresh out of seminary, lent Malka his bicycle.

In modern times, much of institutionalized anti-Semitism arose from old Christian beliefs and superstitions against the Jews that never went away.

Pope Pius XII, head of the Catholic Church during the Holocaust, was famously silent in the face of the extermination of the Jews, of which he was fully aware. On many occasions he would demand that those under his command do nothing to resist Nazi Germany. In a letter that he wrote in the fall of 1941, Pius XII wrote to Konrad von Preysing, who was the bishop of Berlin, "We emphasize that, because the Church in Germany is dependent upon your public behavior... in public declarations you are duty bound to exercise restraint."

To make himself abundantly clear, he reprimanded Konrad von Preysing that Catholic allegiance "requires you and your colleagues not to protest." Incredibly, he even made claims to justify the bloodshed unleashed by Germany upon the world, explaining that Germany was undertaking a noble historical mission of its own.

In one of his most damning letters he admonished that, "Germany is a great nation who, in their fight against Bolshevism, is bleeding not only for their friends but also for the sake of their present enemies."

In other words, Nazi Germany was bleeding for the sake of the British and the Americans and countless others it butchered. No wonder he didn't concern himself with the Jews, who, according to his historical calculus, definitely could not be ranked as a "great nation" like the Germans...

Hence, hundreds of millions of Catholics never heard a single utterance of criticism from their spiritual leader against the perpetrators of the greatest crime against humanity, nor a word in moral support of the victims, let alone a call to actually stand up to the mass slaughter of the Jews. Had he done so, the Nazis probably would have dealt with passive resistance, with lack of cooperation at the very least, from the ordinary folks, who were, for the most part, devout Catholics. Potentially, it could have changed the entire course of events all across the countries where the Catholic Church enjoyed uncontested authority, such as Poland, Spain, Portugal, France, Italy, Western Ukraine, and large swaths of Germany itself.

Had this been the case, Germany would have had a much harder time making its Catholic soldiers blindly follow orders, and what could've had even broader effect – its efforts to execute the Final Solution – most probably would've been halted to a virtual standstill. One can only imagine how different the world would've looked, had the ordinary Polish folks heard their Pope speak up against the massive murder of the Jews.

But Pius XII remained silent, and his silence reverberated all across

Europe, just as he meant it to be. He had no problem with having the Jews, the infidels who rejected his "god," die en masse.

The pontiff of the Catholic church, same as the heads of other churches, was criminally silent in the face of the catastrophe that the Jewish people endured, and many priests picked up his cues and did exactly what the Catholic church has been doing for millennia – from instigating the Crusades to inciting massacres to leading marches of inflamed followers to burn down Jewish ghettos. Only this time it was done in a more modern fashion, by turning a blind eye to the savagery of the Germans and abetting the regular folks who actively assisted the Nazis.

At the same time though, there were quite a few priests and nuns who heeded their individual voice of morality, taking part in the Resistance, hiding Jews in monasteries and villages, using their influence to secure forged papers to help them escape the noose of the Nazi killing machine, smuggling Jews across borders.

Hundreds of these Catholics were sent to concentration camps and executed. Bishop Konrad von Preysing, the one Pius XII admonished in his letter, disobeyed the orders and headed a vast resistance operation in Berlin, in the very heart of the Nazi regime. He was left untouched, due to his high visibility in public eye. One of the many places that hid Jewish children, was an abbey located in Plancherine, not far from Aix-Les-Bains.

But there was a darker side to the story. Thousands of Jewish souls were effectively kidnapped by the church, first taking Jewish children from their desperate parents and sheltering them in a monastery in a disguise of saving their lives, and then brainwashing those innocent souls or outright coercing them into converting to Catholicism.

These were the *tinokos shenishbu*, the babies that were taken hostage, who were denied the opportunity to know their true roots and to follow the faith of their fathers and mothers who perished in the furnace of the Nazi machine. They were purposely "lost track of" so the parents and relatives who survived the war and searched for these children couldn't trace them back. Even after the war was over, more often than not the monasteries did all they could to prevent Jewish children from reuniting with their families and restoring them to their Jewish identity.

※

Malka didn't know the extent of this dark history of the Catholic Church, but she instinctively felt that while showing cordial gratitude, she had to keep a safe distance from a young, friendly priest from Aix-Les-Bains. The empathy he expressed to the Jewish migrants that flooded his town could have meant many things, and she had to stay on alert.

"You can borrow my bike whenever you need," he told Malka with a warm smile and kind eyes. But one never knew what lay behind this appearance. Maybe he was genuinely altruistic and felt sympathy to their plight, and being unable to do much, he was willing to extend small personal favors, like lending his bicycle to a refugee girl approximately his age. But it could be that he hoped to lure this "pure Jewish soul" into his lair, into the dark shadows of the church he swore to serve.

Nevertheless, she was compelled to take him up on the offer that first week they were in Aix-Les-Bains, despite her ambivalence about the sincerity of his intentions. His bicycle offered her transportation to cycle through the countryside, to the homesteads and isolated farms that would hopefully sell her some food.

So off Malka went on her first exploratory expedition, their very first week in Aix-Les-Bains, cycling further and further away, compelled to find some food to buy.

Finally, at a farm over fifteen miles away, she found a farmer willing to sell her a little bit of butter.

It was Friday, Shabbos was soon approaching, and she couldn't continue any further. She was dehydrated and famished when she turned back towards Aix-Les-Bains.

As she began pedaling down the dirt road, the chain of the bicycle broke and fell off. Despondent, hungry, unable to continue, her head pounding, and feeling the pressure of time as the sun began its descent in the sky, she saw that she was in front of an apple orchard, with beautiful, beckoning apples hanging from the low branches that were reaching over a stone wall.

Disheveled and embarrassed, Malka saw a group of men leaning against the wall wearing their French berets pulled forward to protect their eyes from the strong sun shining on them.

"Please," she said to one of them. "Can you sell me a few apples?"

He waved at the tree. "Take as many as you can eat," he answered.

She plucked three or four of them, tucked several of them into her shoulder bag, and gratefully began eating the one in her hand.

The villager who was watching her must have felt pity for the refugee girl, for he kneeled down and fixed the chain on her bicycle, without her asking him to do so, so that she would be able to continue her ride.

Within just a few moments after she ate the apple, her head stopped pounding and she felt her energy returning. Her aching muscles no longer felt as heavy and weak and she felt she had the strength to go on.

*He saved my life*, Malka thought in gratitude.

She offered to pay for more apples, to bring some home for her family, but he wouldn't sell her any more beyond what he had given her. She thanked him profusely for his generosity and help, mounted the bike, and was off. She still had a long way to go, and needed to make it home before Shabbos.

Malka finally reached home just moments before her mother lit the Shabbos candles.

Her siblings surrounded her and asked, "What did you bring?"

She smiled with relief and said, "Some butter and apples,"

"That's wonderful," her sister Sarah said. "We were able to get some bread and someone gave us cocoa."

That was their first Shabbos meal in Les Bains, with bread, butter, three apples and a cup of cocoa.

※

Seeking and finding food was always a challenge, as was having the money to buy it.

Malka continued to borrow the priest's bicycle to ride out to the country on an almost daily basis, including spectacularly beautiful autumn days. She rode up and down the long winding mountain roads covered with fallen leaves of all colors, cycling around the vast vineyards bustling with entire families harvesting grapes into large straw baskets. She cycled through forests filled with the fragrance of spruce trees and ivy, across meadows dotted with berries and mushrooms, up the crests of hills and down the valleys.

Migrant birds often flew above Malka in a triangle formation heading south, as she'd keep on cycling miles and miles on end. Nature was at its most beautiful, awash with trees turning burgundy, orange, yellow, beige and brown colors, the intoxicating, invigorating mountain air touched with a tinge of chill, with birds singing out from above and children shouting each other's names down below in the groves of the vineyards.

Decades later, Malka still recalls the inspiring rustic beauty of the Savoie Alps, and wishes she could go back to take in the rolling vistas of mountains and lakes. But then, in the midst of the battle for the physical survival of her family, she was too worried to enjoy this spectacular beauty.

Her focus was solely dedicated to one mission: finding food. Each time she reached her next destination, another farm, she found the farmer, asked to buy some of his produce, and time and time again she would hear "no" for an answer.

Most of the farmers barely had enough for themselves, and weren't willing to sell. A long winter was waiting for them around the corner, and the uncertainty of the situation in a war torn Europe, the roaming armies that were destroying the fields and seizing any produce they could lay their hands on, spelled a tangible threat of impending hunger.

The government stopped helping the refugees as they were supposed to return to Antwerp once the bombing stopped. Yes, this was true for "regular" Belgian citizens, but not for the Jews whose lives were in dire danger if they walked into the hands of German occupied Antwerp.

The Weinstein's were lucky to avoid too much scrutiny and stay where they were, but they had no way to get any kind of financial aid from the government who viewed them as a threat, a menace to humanity, and even not human beings who deserved to be helped in the face of adversity and danger.

The older girls, Sarah, Malka and Miriam, took turns borrowing the bicycle and riding out to the surrounding farms in almost invariably futile attempts to purchase a little food with the minimal funds they had left.

On one occasion they came back with baked goods that weren't kosher. Still, they bought it, because food was hard currency in those desperate days. They couldn't eat it, but they could barter with it.

But their father ruled that no financial gain could be made from a non-kosher product. So instead they gave it to the young priest as an expression of their appreciation for him lending them his bicycle. In those hungry times, food was worth its weight in gold; it was the best way to repay a kindness.

Electricity became the first luxury they couldn't afford. They resorted to candles, and used them sparingly, with only one candle illuminating the entire room, with everyone huddling around the light. These were days of abject poverty, but when a family comes together to spend a long evening around a solitary candle, there are certain benefits that don't always happen during better times. They were not only in close physical proximity, they felt emotionally close. Their breath in a chilly, dimly lit room added a tiny bit of human warmth. As long as they were together, they had a chance. This was not a thought, but an almost mysterious sense of belonging, deep in their bones.

Staying together, this is what would save their lives.

As their funds ran thin and food prices kept on climbing, they had to do with less, relying on small, rotten potatoes that had to be scrubbed from clumpy chunks of dirt, a carrot or a cabbage and an occasional slice of onion, a few sips of milk diluted in warm water, a plate of watery semolina, or a loaf of coarse dark bread. These were their staples. Butter was long gone. Meat was not even something they could dream about. With cold weather setting in, the vegetables disappeared as well.

That year Rosh Hashanah began on the first days of October. They went to *shul* and it was full, mostly with other refugees from Antwerp. Those few precious days felt almost as if the war hadn't touched them, as they listened to the cantor singing *niggunim,* in the familiar melodies of their hometown that everyone knew. The congregation was full of gratitude, to feel this sense of being home away from home, as they sang the prayers in unison.

And at home, they had saved for the Yom Tov meal the best food they had managed to find, with an extra candle making the room brighter.

※

But there was an undercurrent of unease, of calm before the storm. Rumors and misinformation abounded, some of it planted intentionally by local authorities, adding to the confusion among the refugees.

Some heard that back in Antwerp the occupying German forces were not bothering the Jews too much, and that life continued almost as usual. Some speculated that the Germans were too busy fighting elsewhere, and it would make no sense for them to waste their energy and manpower going after a civilian population. Some hoped that maybe after all was said and done, after all the fiery rhetoric of the madman named Adolf Hitler, at the end of the day the Germans of World War II were not much different from the Germans of the previous Great War. As angry as they might be, they were still the nation of Leibniz and Goethe, of Bach and Beethoven, bound by a common sense of civility. Thinking like this, quite a few refugees returned to Antwerp.

Little did they know that on that very day, on the first day of Rosh Hashanah, October 3, 1940, as their hearts were breaking to pieces together with the wailing sound of the shofar, as they were pouring out their hearts to their Father in Heaven, with their tears streaming down their faces, "*U'teshuvah, u'tefillah, u'tzedakah ma'avirin es ro'ah hagezerah,*" the Loi Portant Statut des Juifs – The Statute on the Jews – was signed into law. For the first time in France's modern history, a legal definition of who was Jewish for the purposes of discrimination and persecution was stipulated. This Statute echoed the Nuremberg Laws of Race.

Jews were prohibited from holding any official position or public office, and Jews of foreign origin, defined as "nomads" and "dangerous elements," were to be accounted for and gathered for further "processing." Bureaucrats are always very good with laundering words...

The following day, an order authorizing the establishment of Internment Camps for Jews who were foreign nationals, was issued. The German High Command in France gave orders to be executed by the French Prefecture, overseen by only a score of German officers.

It took time for the French to get the logistics in place, getting ready to sweep out the Jewish refugees who fled to France. That's probably why it took time for the Statute to get into circulation. The French authorities made sure no one was made aware of the new decree, lest those affected would run and hide and make it harder for the powers that be to execute their policies.

Only two weeks later, on October 18, on the second day of Succos, was the edict entered into official registries, and made public the following day in the newspapers.

Soon after, official notices were pasted up all over town, announcing that Jews of foreign nationality had to gather at Place Maurice Mollard, the central square next to the Town Hall. If they failed to report to the gathering point, they faced the threat of death penalty.

Despite the ominous language, the refugees didn't really take it too seriously. At a moment of distress, people have a tendency to come up with all the possible and impossible excuses to explain what is happening. It would be unprecedented to kill people just for not showing up, they reasoned. The French were always known for their fondness for hyperbole and literary exaggeration, others speculated. Weren't they a civil nation after all? The soft-hearted, liberty loving French just couldn't be capable of such an atrocity.

This same rationale caused millions of people to stay put, all across Western and Central and Eastern Europe, awaiting their terrible fate, hearing but not believing, understanding the words but refusing to internalize their lethal meaning. People just couldn't believe that reality could be so strikingly, improbably horrific. Confirmation bias was probably the leading fatality factor in the history of the Holocaust...

Granted, not everyone complied. Some, who had enough money to continue renting their villas and buying food at exorbitant prices, took their chances in evading the deportation notice, figuring they'd keep a low profile until the wheel of fortune turned.

However, most of the Jews who took refuge in Aix-Les-Bains went to the square that fateful day. The government was no longer providing a stipend for the refugees, and most of them had used up their limited resources on the scarce food available. They were too emotionally worn down to continue resisting the inevitable. Either way, they had no money to board a train and sneak out of the tightening noose. On the other hand, they had no desire to find out how serious the French were about the death penalty hyperbole they were toying with.

This was also the reason why the Weinstein's didn't do what they did in Montesquieu and run for their lives. Like a gazelle, after it has galloped for endless miles, finally runs out of its last drop of strength and collapses in the grass, surrendering to the mercy of her pursuers, so it was with the Weinstein's and many others. They stepped out of the shadows on that cold, windy morning and went to the town square of a once charming Aix-Les-Bains, to face their fate.

CHAPTER SEVEN

# D'agde: The Night When Angels Came

NOVEMBER 1940

On that morning, the Jews converged on Place Maurice Mollard, the main square facing the Town Hall. Only when they entered the square did they notice that it was cordoned off by the French gendarmerie, blocking all side streets and entrances to the buildings that could be used as escape routes. With nowhere to go, the Jews squeezed between the Town Hall and the Astoria Palace flanking the square.

The neighboring streets, bombed by the Luftwaffe less than five months prior, lay in ruins, rendering the place a dystopian feel of apocalypse. Children, frightened, huddled to their parents. They screamed when a horse-mounted French gendarme plowed through the crowd, as if to show them that he deemed them non-existent.

They were sitting on the pavement, waiting for eternity, as it seemed. At last the police Prefect gave the order, and gendarmes broke the Jews up into square formations, lined them in columns, and marched them to Gare d'Aix-Les-Bains-Le Revard, the train station a mere five hundred yards away.

The train carried a freshly minted insignia of SNCF, Société Nationale des Chemins de Fer Français, the National Society of Railroads of France. SNCF, a patchwork of regional railroads all across France, was comprised of a number of private and public companies that, by decree of 1938, only two years before, was restructured as a state-owned company, and stood at the service of the French government. The Armistice of 1940 placed the French rail system directly under German transport command. When French authorities chose to deport people, the rail company had no way to say no.

Following orders, the Weinstein's left everything behind. All the meager possessions they managed to keep ever since they fled Antwerp, they couldn't bring along with them. The stark unknown, the sheer terror of being displaced and dispossessed, and taken to an unknown destination toward an unknown future decided by those who loathe your very existence, stared them in the face.

The last time they took the train, when fleeing Antwerp, they took it on their own accord, making their own decision. As frightening as it had been the first time around, they made that choice and they knew where they were going.

Not this time.

However, the Weinstein's were lucky to take that train. True, their destination was Camp d'Agde, an internment camp in southeast France with harsh, deadly conditions. But it was nowhere near the fate the remainder of the Jews of Aix-Les-Bains would have to face. The few hundred who stayed behind, unaffected by the Statute on the Jews, thanks to their good fortunes of being naturally born French citizens, were deported three years later, on July 13, 1943. Their terminal destination was not Camp d'Agde, but a small town in south Poland called Oswiecim, renamed by the Germans as Auschwitz...

The old regional train rattled, took off and slowly pulled out of the station. It headed south, plowing its way through forests and mountain ridges, across bridges and over deep valleys, down to Grenoble. Locked in train cars, they waited on the reserve tracks in the middle of nowhere, then took off again and continued southwest toward Valenca where they waited more. Then they picked up speed heading south toward Avignon, and kept on rolling slowly to the west again. At last they passed Montpellier and rolled on a very narrow strip of land separating the Mediterranean Sea on the left from Étang de Thau, a lagoon stretching for fifteen miles alongside the coastal line. Then they entered the outskirts of Agde, crossed the bridge over the

Hérault River, and crawled to Gare d'Agde, the train station of Agde, their final destination.

Today this trip from Aix-Les-Bains would take four to five hours. In those days of calamity and chaos, the journey took much, much longer.

Like Gurs, the Internment Camp at Agde was originally built by military engineers in 1939, on land belonging to the Agde municipality, to serve as a receiving center for Spanish Republican refugees who fled to France after the defeat of the Spanish revolution. Intended for fifteen to twenty thousand people, in July 1939, it already swelled to holding over twenty-four thousand refugees. The camp included approximately two hundred wooden barracks, sprawling on a patch of land of about thirty acres. After having cleared most of Spanish refugees, it was used to house different military regiments, from one thousand Czech volunteers who came to fight Nazi Germany, to military conscripts from Belgium who, on the day their home country capitulated to Germany, had their status turned into detainees.

On October 25, 1940, Camp d'Agde administration was transferred directly under the Vichy Interior Ministry, and assumed the official name of "Reception Center for Foreigners." Soon it held almost six thousand civilian detainees, from thirty different nationalities, of which one thousand were Jews, who, like the Weinstein's, were mostly from Belgium. Or there were Jews from Germany, who, under the new Statute on the Jews, were deemed "dangerous elements" and a "threat" to the French republic.

※

As the train halted to a stop at Gare d'Agde, the deportees were ordered to disembark, arranged in columns resembling forced labor battalions, and filed through the city center and over the bridge, crossing again the Herault River. They were heading toward the Internment Camp, situated to the northeast of Agde. The newly arrived detainees were corralled into Camp IV, allocated for civilians, and further separated to Sub-camps. Women and children under the age of twelve were incarcerated in Sub-camps 1 and 2, and men were sent to Sub-camps 3 and 3a.

Esther and her children all found themselves in the same barrack, along with other mothers and young children.

After the ordeal of the last twenty-four hours, Malka was relieved to lie down on the narrow cots and eat the meager portion of food that they were given. *This is good,* she thought. *We might be in captivity, but we are together, we have a place to lay our heads, and I won't need to desperately search for food every single day, cycling around.*

Yet conditions were miserable. No running water, which meant severe sanitation and hygiene problems. No heating or electricity in the barracks. The camp was so underfunded that frequently the suppliers wouldn't be paid and they stopped providing food, and prisoners would go hungry for days.

There was constant chaos, but at least the guards left the Jews alone. The French still hadn't figured out what they were going to do with all the prisoners they were amassing. They were so confused about their own policies and the discipline was so lax, that at first it was still possible to leave the camp for a few hours with the proper permit, which accounted for frequent escapes. The Prefect of the local police even noted in his letter to the Ministry of Interior that the guards in the camp were "powerless to stop this exodus."

There wasn't much to do all day. The children often watched the Czech volunteers and Belgian demobilized conscripts exercising daily in the adjacent camp II. Chaim Yair was even allowed to visit his family during the day, returning to his barracks in the evening.

Weeks stretched into months, with conditions only deteriorating. The roofs leaked and the thin walls made of wooden planks didn't protect them from the fierce winds blowing in from the sea. When winter began in earnest, snowdrifts mounded up under their beds.

One day there was a visitor to the barracks, a tall, modestly dressed woman, who they later learned was Madame Aron. She met with the women in the barracks, and was clearly pained by their misery. Kind and courteous, her attention was quickly drawn to the Weinstein family. She came over to speak with them at length, and Berel's infirmity tugged at her heartstrings. Esther's outspoken resolve to care for her nine children in the squalid conditions of the camp left a deep impression on her. They soon discovered that she was quite an influential personality. Her husband, Monsieur Aron Lourié, was Treasurer-General of OSE-ORT in Montpellier.

'Œuvre de Secours aux Enfants,' Children's Aid Society, abbreviated as OSE, was first established by Jewish doctors in Saint Petersburg, Russia in 1912, with a goal of providing relief to Jewish communities stricken by war, anti-Semitism, and pogroms that plagued Russia. Following the devastation that came in the wake of the Great War, OSE opened branches in Poland, Romania, Lithuania, and Latvia. In 1923, soon after the Bolsheviks staged a revolution and a bloody civil war swept Russia, the headquarters moved to Berlin. When Hitler, the worst predator monster of the twentieth century, ascended to power in 1933, OSE relocated once again, to Paris.

In 1935, in response to the influx of refugees from Germany, Austria and Czechoslovakia, OSE merged with ORT.* ORT was another major Jewish relief organization established in Russia back in 1880 with a goal of creating vocational training centers and providing Jews with needed skills to pursue high-skilled trades or learn to live off the land. After the Communist revolution in Russia in 1917, ORT also escaped the civil war and set up its headquarters in Paris in 1921.

Together, OSE and ORT established a joint venture called "The Child Rescue and Health Protection of Jewish Populations," which become the official name of the Union in France. Heads of the OSE-ORT probably had a better strategic and military vision than the heads and the marshals of the French Republic. They did not believe that the Line of Maginot would shield France from the German Wehrmacht, and made necessary preparations prior to the Fall of France. The OSE-ORT Union branched out into two parts, one operating out of Paris, and the other one, assigned to Vichy France, relocated to Montpellier, with M. Aron Lourié as the Treasurer-General.

This organization, highly esteemed for its humanitarian work during the times of prosperity and progress of the Third French

---

* Acronym of a Russian title: "Obschestvo Remeslenno-zemledelcheskogo Truda" – The Society for Trades and Agricultural Labour.

Republic, still commanded great respect from French officials, even under German occupation and in Vichy France. Madame Aron Lourié used her influence and arranged for two families to be released, the Weinstein family being one of them.

She saved their lives.

In 1942, all the Jews remaining in Camp d'Agde, including those from Antwerp, were deported to Rivesaltes, Noé and Drancy, and eventually to Auschwitz, where they were sent directly to the ovens.

⁂

The Weinstein's were free, as free as one can be, belonging to a hunted down race in the heart of war-ravaged Europe. Madame Aron Lourié procured forged identity cards and food rations for them. Then she rented a small cottage for them in Prades-le-Lez, a quaint community not far from Agde, just eight miles north of Montpellier.

With new documents, they were now legally in France, and could move around without fear. But that was not all. Madame Lourié secured a small stipend for them from the United Jewish Appeal (UJA), which granted them enough provisions to allow them to get by.

This woman was an angel in human form, though she, too, and her husband, had their own share of suffering. Their seventeen year-old daughter, an only child, was crippled by polio. But Madame Lourié never complained. All she did was help others, in any way she could. Besides saving the Weinstein's from sure death, she gave them a chance to live, day in and day out.

It was an odd, uncomfortable, even uncanny, feeling. How do you take a stroll down the street without always seeing barbed wire blocking your way, without fearing, at least for the time being, the reprisals, the roundups, the impending deportation? How do you wake up in the morning having food, not needing to worry that you are going to go hungry today?

It was nothing short of a miracle.

But it was a mixed blessing. The rescue came not without a great share of survivor's guilt. In a reality where a person's true self inevitably is revealed, and many painful life and death choices are being made, where mistakes that cost a life could happen in a moment, almost no one escaped unscathed.

During the long listless weeks and months in Camp d'Agde, Malka made many friends, but as she walked out a free person, they remained there, behind the barbed wire, and the chances that they would ever meet again dwindled by the day. As the situation deteriorated and repressions against *indésirables*, especially Jews, became more mainstream and were applied with more stringency, virtually no one attempted to escape any longer.

Even the local rabbi, reasoning that he was doing what he had to do to deflect the wrath of the new regime from his community, promised the authorities that if any of the foreign born Jews incarcerated at Camp d'Agde escaped and came to him for shelter, he would bring them back. And he kept his word.

When a local priest would incite his congregants against the Jews, it was not shocking. He did what his predecessors were doing for hundreds of years. But when a rabbi, who was supposed to be a beacon of spiritual clarity and moral compass, made a pact with his own conscience and compromised his moral and spiritual integrity, it was a true blow to any faith in people. If you can't trust a rabbi to save you, who else can you trust? A total stranger? A non-Jew, who you can't expect to care? Losing faith in another person is sometimes the worst side effect of being a victim. Victims aren't only in pain from injury they sustain. They also feel they lose their instinct to understand what's good and what's evil, their ability to trust others or even themselves. Either they or the world went mad, or both.

Why even try to escape, if all that awaits you out there in a big open world is betrayal? Why even live, if adversity bared the true nature of human beings and betrayal has become the rule of the land? There were rumors of valiant men and women who stood by their conscience and even heroically paid with their lives, but who ever met them? Do people like that live next to us? Can we be people like that, or we are destined to live as cowards and die as traitors? If even a rabbi can be a traitor, if even our faith doesn't make us more courageous, what will?

But then there was Madame Aron Lourié. She was not born into a religious home and she married an assimilated Jew like herself. She came closer to *Yiddishkeit* and became a practicing Jew, while her husband remained secular. But they trusted each other and both dedicated their lives to saving other Jewish lives, irrespective of their personal religious beliefs. They were a ray of life in that dark, dark world.

※

One day the Weinstein's faced their own moral dilemma. Malka's old classmate Ruth, from Antwerp, who was also deported to Camp d'Agde, tried her luck and escaped. Taking the enormous risk of being caught, she walked and hitch-hiked the narrow dirt side roads of the Hérault department, making her way from Agde to the west, making sure to stay clear of a major city like Montpellier, where too many eyes were watching.

Finally she reached and entered Prades-le-Lez. She searched for and found the house the Weinstein's were staying in and knocked on the door. Esther welcomed her in and offered her food to eat, just like she used to do in the good old days of life in Antwerp.

So here she was, a young girl Malka's age, with nowhere to go, asking if she could join them.

It was a dreadful moment. As much as they wanted to help, the Weinstein's felt they had nothing to offer. She didn't have any documents on her, and their own situation, with false identities, a cover that could be blown any moment, was precarious. They didn't know how long they could stay. They didn't know when that inevitable moment would come when they would have to drop everything and make their rapid escape.

It was not a question of "if" but of "when" they would find themselves on the run again, and they didn't even have the faintest idea where they would be going. Their lives could be upended in a split second...it was only a question of time.

This young girl didn't have any false identity papers that would give her a chance to cross a border, to board a train, enter a store or even any public place... Taking in another person could jeopardize their own mobility, and ultimately... their chance of survival.

It was very difficult to express all this to Ruth.

Heavy, unbearable silence descended on the room as she was making her way to the door.

They have no idea where Ruth went. She never returned. Malka remained haunted by the expression on Ruth's face that changed from despair to resigned, eyes looking at her, a girl she left behind and who probably didn't survive. Those sad eyes looked at her for months, for years, and for the decades that followed.

The ORT school vocational training in Montpellier was located nine miles away. The schooling was free, funded by the UJA. Malka enrolled and learned the art of dressmaking, from nine in the morning until one in the afternoon. She soon discovered that she had natural talent in this area. After school her teacher Mademoiselle Muller, a professional dressmaker who had fled from Paris, brought Malka and a few other classmates with her to help her sew dresses for private clients. They didn't earn much from this work, but every *centime* helped.

Under the new racial laws, regular public schools wouldn't admit Jewish children, and even though dressmaking was a promising and comparatively convenient trade and she even excelled at it, every morning Malka fantasized about a day when she'd wake up and get dressed and walk out of her house and then instead of taking up a seat behind a table with a thread and a needle in her hand, she'd go to a real school and open a book and study. She missed real education, which was so abruptly ended. *If I ever get out of this, I'm going to go to school no matter what*, she vowed to herself.

The commute to Montpellier was grueling. Malka decided to board with an elderly Jewish woman, whose son was active in the OSE. The woman needed company, and gave Malka a place to stay in return.

As the weeks passed, the family settled in the village. Years later, Naftoli remembered that time fondly. For him, in his memories, it felt like they were on a kind of vacation. He'd go with his father every Shabbos to *toivel* in a stream in the forest. Children always live in the moment, and the natural beauty of the lush woodlands that surrounded the small community, with streams and meadows and rivers, made Naftoli feel so absolutely carefree and simply happy, as only a child could be, splashing in water with his father, unaware of the threat of war that permeated Europe.

On one memorable occasion, Naftoli was horrified by a large snake sliding towards them. His father grabbed a stick and hit the snake and it slithered away. Naftoli was in such awe of how brave and strong his father was that now he was absolutely confident that life was as safe as it can be...

The war progressed and Europe drowned in further chaos. Country folks were recruited to frontlines, crops and cattle were destroyed or expropriated by the Germans, roads and railways were flooded with military machinery and troops, and produce became scarce. Food shortages became a real concern, so that even when the store was open, the food tickets didn't always guarantee that there was anything available to exchange them for.

The local bakery gave them a little extra bread in exchange for their meat tickets which they couldn't use anyway. But as the war progressed, the rationing tightened. As they had done in Aix-Les-Bains, Sarah and Miriam again began spending their days scouting the nearby homesteads searching for food they could buy to supplement their meager diets.

They went to nearby farms, hoping the farmers would have a few extra apples or potatoes, or a little butter or milk that they'd be willing to sell.

Sarah had matured into a very determined young woman, with an assertive character and a great deal of confidence to make decisions when needed.

Their father often had to remain in hiding. Although they were in France legally, he was reluctant to shave off his beard, and it marked him as a Jew and an easy target for deportation. With time, the balance of power slightly shifted in the family, and Sarah grew into a de facto leader of the family in those challenging years, calling the shots in the ever shifting landscape of war. Miriam, her partner and right hand, was also a strong, intelligent girl, who was more than willing to be a team player. She had a habit of calling everyone "gorgeous," and her siblings teased her by calling her "gorgeous" back. *Yiddishkeit* meant a great deal to her, and she was scrupulous with *mitzvos* as much as she could be.

She wasn't detached from reality; she was immersed in how to make the best of their lives. She made a strong impression as being every bit down to earth, with a very realistic take on reality. She was grateful for the good while simultaneously grappling with the bad, taking on challenges when the circumstances called for her to do so.

Sarah and Miriam were a duo of sojourners foraging for their big family, day after day. Sometimes they were lucky to find food and sometimes not. They still had no idea of the depravation that was going on in the concentration camps and the extent of the inhumane cruelty that existed. Instead they faced the callousness of local people lashing out during harsh times, when everyone was dealing with hunger and starvation.

Sarah, in particular, felt responsible for her parents and younger siblings who were depending on them to find some food to relieve their persistent hunger. Needing to fight the struggles of the daily battle on the treacherous roads and at the same time feeling responsible for the physical survival of so many people, took a toll on her.

Years later, Sarah described how difficult and stressful it was. She hid it at the time and made everyone – including herself – believe that it was more like an adventure, and an exercise in cheerful resourcefulness that came effortlessly to her. But deep inside her, she felt that it was wearing her down, mentally and emotionally.

Years later she could still feel the burden of those long gone days, the tension, the sheer fear of gnawing danger, weighing heavily on her.

CHAPTER EIGHT

# Knocking on Heaven's Door: From Château de Masgelier to Montpellier Hospital

FEBRUARY 1941

Food was running out. Sarah and Miriam went faithfully day in and day out to forage for food, but the little they managed to return with wasn't even close to enough to feed a family of nine. A community leader in Montpellier, the son of the old woman Malka boarded with, was part of the OSE committee, which transitioned from a highly visible and venerated humanitarian organization at the very heart of the civil life of the French Third Republic, into a sprawling underground network of safe houses and smuggling operations in the midst of German occupied France.

This man in Montpellier was one of the activists doing whatever could be done to save lives.

As soon as the war broke out, being realistic about the capabilities of the French military and its morale, heads of the OSE knew that the fall of France was imminent, only an issue of time. It turned out to be a mere six weeks. Acting on their assessment, they evacuated the four Children's Homes they ran in the Paris Region to different communities in the Creuse department, in the very heartland of France. Taking the Germans' word of making the world Judenrein, the OSE opened a slew of clandestine nurseries and homes to hide

Jewish children from their inevitable fate. The OSE were indiscriminate in their policies. They'd take in children of any age and any walk of life, from totally secular to strictly religious, from all across France.

The OSE did everything they could to diversify the risk and make sure that even if one fortress fell, others had a chance to make an escape. They had safe houses set up in the very heart of central France – solitary castles Château de Masgelier near Grand-Bourg, Château de Chaumont on the outskirts of Mainsat, and an old townhome lined on a small street in a village of Chabannes (part of today's Saint-Pierre-de-Fursac), in the heart of the Creuse region. A few more were set up in Limoges and Montintin in the Haute-Vienne region, and in Brout-Vernet in the Allier, right outside of Vichy, the seat of the pro-German government. The OSE crisscrossed France in search of safe homes, even renting places as far southwest as Couret, a tiny hamlet of barely a hundred inhabitants in the Midi-Pyrénées region, near the Franco-Spanish border.

Even in their school programming, the OSE proved how brutally realistic they were. They instructed the teachers to put a special emphasis on physical agility and survival skills, making sure to prepare their young students for the worst that was yet to come. Parents of many of the children they were hiding were either caught already or about to get rounded up and find themselves on their way to deportation, facing their bitter end at the concentration camps. The OSE tried to do all they could to give the children they saved a fighting chance, some chance at least, whatever the future held in store for them.

"Send your children to one of our safe homes," he urged Chaim Yair. "They'll be looked after, will have enough food to eat, and learn. It's a religious home and your children will be well taken care of."

Faced with the looming threat of starvation, Chaim Yair agreed. Until now their family had survived, and they all credited it to the fact that they did all they could to stay together. Now he was told to break up the family, and a heavy foreboding made this decision a truly painful one. But with every passing day their options were dwindling. They were running out of resources, and he knew he had to act. When the next opportunity presented itself, he did what he had to do.

One Friday morning, the three younger children – Leah, Yankel, and Naftoli – climbed into the back of a truck that was traveling to Montpellier. From there they set out on a long voyage to Château de Masgelier, a remote mansion near Grand-Burg, in the department of Creuse, three hundred and twenty miles away.

Château de Masgelier looked like a castle from a fairy tale. Situated on a hilltop, with panoramic views over the Creuse countryside, and set within its own parkland, the Chateau du Masgelier dated from the end of the twelfth century. One of the oldest and most historic medieval castles in the Limousin, with a colorful history dating back to the Knights Templar, it was originally built as a hilltop defense castle and still retained its vast walled battlements. The sprawling, two story mansion with a medieval tower on the corner and a stately marble double staircase, was surrounded by enormous grounds and woods. A long tree-lined avenue led up to its arched gate. It was a magical hideaway from all the evil in the world.

The couple that ran the place, Hélène and Jacques Bloch, had come from Russia as a part of the OSE original organization. They were inspired by the work of Dr. Janusz Korczak, a Jewish pioneer of humanistic education who established an orphanage in Warsaw, Poland. Dr. Janusz was later given the option to escape but instead chose to share the fate of the children he sheltered and raised. He chose to die together with them in the Treblinka gas chambers.

The Bloch's cared for these refugee children with great devotion, instilling in them a sense of empowerment and self-respect. All the adults running the place ate together with the children in a large dining room. The little children felt free to climb into the lap of their teacher, who was more of a mother figure than a stern disciplinarian, giving them the love they were cruelly bereft of.

Their education did not involve a formal, rigorous, academic curriculum. The atmosphere was more like that of a summer camp, with plenty of time spent playing, but also acquiring essential skills to survive in the forest. They spent hours learning to plant vegetables and dig ditches to hide in; how to make a fire in a pit so that it could not be seen from afar; to find and hook worms to use for bait to catch fish, and then how to scale and clean the fish and cook them.

They went into the forest to learn how to identify and discern edible mushrooms, plants and berries from poisonous ones. They learned how to sustain themselves through real life experience.

The focus was on Jewish survival, no matter what. And if they did indeed survive the war, then in the future they could pursue more formal education and learn professions.

On Pesach they were all given a portion of matzah to eat for the Seder. Only later were they able to appreciate what an effort it took to make this matzah: finding wheat that was not soaked in water, having it ground especially for matzah; baking it according to all the requirements of *halachah,* and then giving it to children younger than the age of bar – and bat mitzvah, who, from a strictly *halachic* requirement, didn't even have a Torah obligation to eat matzah in the first place.

People at OSE truly put their lives on the line to preserve not only the physical, but also the spiritual survival of these Jewish children, who were pursued relentlessly by the Nazi war machine.

When the younger children were in Le Masgelier for several days, and Malka was home for the weekend, visiting her family, her mother asked her to please check with her landlady's son if he had any news from the children.

"When you are back there, please find out how they are doing," she begged her daughter.

When Malka returned to ORT, as soon as she had an opportunity to see her landlady's son, she didn't have a chance to ask her question, when he tersely said, "An ambulance took your brother to the hospital. You need to bring your father or mother right away. Your brother is not doing well."

"Oh no! There is only one bus back to my parents, and it leaves at six o'clock in the morning. I won't be able to reach them until tomorrow! I will go to the hospital immediately!'"

She hurried there, praying in her heart that it wasn't little Naftoli. Yankel was definitely stronger, while Naftoli was so small and frail, his chances of survival from whatever it was that had happened to him, much slimmer than his older siblings.

But when she arrived, she found it was him, Naftoli, lying in the enormous hospital bed, unresponsive. He appeared to be even smaller than his six years. He looked so weak, his face pale and wreathed with pain. It was shocking to see him this way.

"What happened? What's wrong with him?" Malka asked the nurse that was in the room changing the bandages that were wrapped around his abdomen.

"The doctor will explain," she answered.

Malka didn't want to leave her brother to find the doctor. "Please, tell me what happened. Why are there bandages on him?"

The nurse was about to answer when the doctor entered the room and said, "He arrived a few days ago, in excruciating pain, with a burst infected appendix. The bacteria spread to his entire abdominal area. He has peritonitis, which means the infection is virulent. I'm sorry to say, but we don't have much with which to treat him. We can only hope that his immune system will be able to fight off the infection before it spreads to his vital organs and causes a complete systemic failure."

He meant that her brother could die!

"You need to get your parents," the doctor continued. "Your brother is very, very sick. His situation is precarious."

"I can't get them, they don't live here! It's a long journey..." Malka began to say. "I can't go until tomorrow morning."

And she couldn't leave Naftoli alone.

She stayed up all night saying *tehillim*, praying for her little brother to survive.

In the morning she decided she would go to the post office to call her parents, and not travel to the village. She had to stay with her brother.

Making a phone call wasn't a simple task; it was a long tedious procedure beginning by going to the post office, making a reservation for a phone line that would be managed by switch operators at calling centers, coordinating calls that had to be processed through the one existing line running from one town to the next. In small villages this could all take many hours or the whole day.

When morning came, she quietly left Naftoli, who still didn't even know she was there with him. She went to the post office, got in line to make a reservation and then waited patiently until it was her turn.

When the operator reached the post office in the village where her parents lived, Malka begged the clerk on the phone to find a boy outside on the street who could go and inform her parents that they must come back to the post office and call her back.

She knew that as soon as the messenger appeared to get them, they would know something was terribly wrong.

Finally, her parents called back. They were allotted barely a minute to communicate on a line that crackled with static, as though the words were traveling underwater in a stormy sea, threatening to break up at any moment.

They were horrified to hear the news.

"Is he still alive? When did you last see him? What did the doctors say? What is his prognosis?" The questions stumbled out, with that most terrible question uppermost in their minds.

Malka didn't know the answer.

"I will contact the hospital and then I will call you back," she reassured her parents.

The clerk at the post office was kind enough to give her a line to the phone operator who connected her with the hospital. And then she was allowed to use the phone booth again for the out-of-town call.

"You can only speak for about thirty seconds," the clerk reminded her.

When Malka reached the nurse, she said, "Yes, so far, he's holding his own. We're hoping the crisis is over."

She quickly called back her parents and relayed the news.

"We need to keep praying!" she said, and then hung up and went back to the hospital to spend the day at Naftoli's bedside.

To keep diseases from being transmitted, contact between patients and visitors was restricted and visiting hours were often completely ruled out. But Naftoli was a little boy who needed a family member there to take care of him, so Malka was allowed to sit next to him, but not to touch him.

He was lying there on a bed that looked disproportionately large for his tiny frame, too weak to open his eyes, drifting in and out of consciousness, his body battling the infection. He looked exhausted, fragile and so vulnerable.

Malka wasn't even sure Naftoli knew she was next to him. She wished she could hold his tiny fingers, so that he would feel that someone who loved him was there right beside him.

But she knew better to not even entertain such a thought, otherwise she would be told to leave at once. The surgical wound was left intentionally open so that the puss, instead of staying inside and spreading through the tissue, would drip out of the abdominal cavity. The nurse came every once in a while to wipe the area with alcohol, which caused Naftoli to wince with pain.

Tears stood in his eyes, but he didn't dare to cry out loud. He was just a little boy, taken care of by adults, and he had to be quiet even if it hurt. He didn't know why, he only knew they had to do this. They tried all they could to make sure the infection wouldn't spread.

Malka felt as if time froze. She was anxious for her parents to come. They wouldn't come until the next afternoon, when the first bus from Prades-le-Lez would finally arrive in Montpellier.

But how could they come? It was still too risky for her father to appear in public. It was safer in the out-of-the-way countryside, whereas Montpellier was a comparatively big city, with a substantial presence of police and military always on the streets. Their father couldn't risk being caught and interned in camps again.

And her mother, she knew, couldn't come either. Caring for the house and trying to turn scraps of scarce produce into something edible to feed her children to prevent them from dying from starvation consumed all her time and strength. Sarah and Miriam, her older, responsible daughters usually weren't home to watch their younger siblings. They were searching for food in the outlying areas.

Though their father could have watched the children, she still couldn't leave, for a more painful reason.

She was too broken.

Their harrowing escape, almost having lost her husband, the deportation, the incarceration – her heart was broken, and her inner strength was barely accessible for her to go through the motions of daily life. She was weak and sickly... and to see her little boy suffering, in agony, with no guarantee that he would survive the ordeal, would be too much for her to endure.

The doctor confirmed what it was: peritonitis, appendicitis that burst and infected the entire abdominal area. They had removed the appendix and drained the intestinal area, but now Naftoli suffered from a widespread infection.

The required cleansing of the operation site with alcohol a few times a day was an excruciating procedure. But this was the only treatment they could offer for an internal infection.

Either Naftoli's immune system would be able to fight off the infection and his white cells would devour the pathogenic bacteria, or the infection would spread to vital organs, causing systemic failure, and then Naftoli wouldn't survive...

Naftoli's life was in limbo, and the medical staff at the Montpellier hospital couldn't offer any assurances.

He got sick a few years too early. A few years prior, in a revolutionary clinical trial in Oxford, the first patient was cured with a whole new kind of miracle medicine extracted from a mold. The medicine was called "penicillin," after the mildew it was extracted from. This new revolutionary type of medication was named "antibiotics," for its amazing property of killing bacteria that cause disease. But many years of repeated clinical trials and failures had passed until it was successfully used in hospital settings on several burn patients who developed infections, in 1942, a year after Naftoli fell ill with peritonitis.

On top of it, this medical wonder took place not in Europe but across the Atlantic, in Boston, Massachusetts. Moreover, the means for mass production of this miracle drug weren't developed until June

1945, just after the war ended. In those pre-antibiotic days, recovering was a long and tedious process.

❦

When the day ended, the nurse asked Malka to leave for the night and come the next morning.

As Malka looked at Naftoli, his breath labored, his hair damp on the pillow, his features so sharp and small, a defenseless child being devoured by a microscopic monster, her heart skipped a beat.

Would her brother survive the night? Would she see him tomorrow, alive?

The next morning she was there as soon as visitors were allowed in. She continued to sit by Naftoli's bed. When the doctor came to evaluate Naftoli she was asked to wait outside his room.

Overwhelmed by the need to know what was happening, she peeked in the door, and whispered, "How's my brother?" The doctor was not pleased to be bothered by this foreign girl.

"Talk to the nurse," he retorted. His curt answer petrified her. *Why did he answer like that? Did the situation worsen and the doctor doesn't want to tell her?*

Malka felt like the floor was sliding out from underneath her, but she had to hold her ground. Then the nurse came out and said, "Your brother survived the night, and his fever went down, which is a great sign." She said these words with a reassuring voice. Malka felt like crying from the huge relief she suddenly felt wash over her.

Small for his age and malnourished from the ordeal of hunger, his body had little strength to battle. It took longer than usual for him to recuperate, to be able to climb out of bed, to regain weight, and to walk again. Every morning, when Naftoli was in pain, silently crying during the excruciating procedure of cleaning up the incision, the internist would reassure him.

"It will be alright," he would say, stroking his hair. "It will be alright."

Slowly, very slowly, the swelling subsided, and Naftoli improved enough to be able to eat solid food, not just the semolina or the watery soup that he learned to hate with a passion, which was the only food he was allowed to eat. Eventually, when he was strong enough, Malka brought him some bread and fruit, and it was a true feast.

She came every day during the breaks from school, between noon and three p.m. in the afternoon. Naftoli waited for her anxiously, the only family he had in this big foreign place. Though the nurses, with their big white hats and white aprons treated him kindly, he was just one of many, a little boy from nowhere in an overwhelming ocean of sickness and suffering.

He slept in a large hall, with dozens of beds lined up in rows like in a military barrack, with a narrow passage between the two rows. There weren't separate rooms for children and curtains between beds to offer individuals any privacy. Patients of all ages and with all kinds of diseases were lying next to him. Some were delirious, some had amputated limbs, screaming in pain after a surgery; some were retching and hallucinating, and some were dying. In the morning, men would come and carry away those who died during the night.

There was one other Jewish boy in the ward with him. They became friends, sitting on the same bed, playing with buttons that they lined up as soldiers. They pretended they were the generals fighting the Germans.

Three long grueling months passed that Naftoli remained in the hospital, fighting the infection.

When Naftoli was finally officially released from the hospital, Malka brought Naftoli home to Prades-le-Lez, but he was still very weak. His sunken eyes were filled with an unmistakable trace of resignation. He was pale and unsteady on his feet. But he and his entire family were happy that he was alive and they were reunited.

It was a true miracle that Naftoli had survived the dangerous inflammation and the surgery, and didn't catch any of the infectious diseases that were ravaging countless victims on the frontlines and in the hospitals.

The Weinstein's organized a *seudah hodayah* in honor of their son who had miraculously survived invasive surgery, raging inflammation and life-threatening infection. One of the highlights of the *seudah* was his ability to eat the grapes that were served in his honor. Grapes were a staple food abundant in southern France that he had not been allowed to eat while his digestive system was so inflamed and sensitive.

---

Only after he fully recovered was he able to endure the three hundred and twenty mile trip in the back of a truck rattling through muddy ditches in winding country roads to return to Grand-Bourg in central France where Château de Masgelier was located. During that trip, his stitches hurt and he felt nauseous and dizzy, but he had learned in his three month hospital stay that there was no one to complain to, he had to hold on tight, and endure eight hours on the road.

He arrived at Château de Masgelier close to Shabbos, but with enough time to bathe and change into new clothes. The clothes he was wearing were filthy with dirt and dust from the long trip.

But he had no clothes to change into.

With her dressmaking skills, his sister Malka was able to alter his pants, but altering a shirt was a much more complicated task and the only shirt he had was the one on his back.

Another boy, seeing the distress and embarrassment on the face of the vulnerable youth who had just arrived, went over to Naftoli and said, "Don't worry about your shirt, I can lend you one of mine."

Naftoli looked up, touched that anyone had noticed him. The physical sensation of a clean shirt, its soft, almost delicate touch, was so different from the creased, worn out one he had on his body for so many weeks. It was such a delight, mixed with the heartfelt gratitude toward the boy who had been so generous to him, a strange boy who he didn't even know, who befriended him on his first day there.

Many years later, he'd still have that sensory memory, of a soft fabric touching his skin, and the sweet gratefulness sweeping his heart. He remembered that moment his entire life.

CHAPTER NINE

# *From Castle to Cabin: Nantes-en-Ratier*

JANUARY 1942

Almost two years passed since the family escaped the ruins of Antwerp. The children were happy in camp, safe and well fed. Naftoli had fully recovered. There seemed no reason to change anything. Chaim Yair couldn't explain the sudden urge that took hold of him. Just like back at the train station near Gurs, his gut feeling told him he had to act, immediately, to get ahead of the game that some invisible hand was playing against him. "Sarah," he began to say to his daughter. "Please go get your siblings. They need to come home right now."

Sarah stared at her father's expression and went straight out of their home to search for the person who first sent them there.

When she found him, she said, "My father wants the children home. Now."

"Are you crazy? Why? They have food. They're happy. They're enjoying themselves."

"I don't ask questions," Sarah said. "If my father wants them back, we trust his intuition. All I know is that he wants them back."

"You want the children? Take them," the community leader was fuming. "But it's madness. Absolute madness."

"That's a matter of opinion," Sarah tried to speak softly. "We are so grateful for everything you did for us! But my father decided this and we trust him, and I have to do what he told me to do. Could you please make sure they get on the first truck that travels from Château de Masgelier to Montpellier? We'll pick them up as soon as they are here."

She could feel the tension in the air as he seemed to be wavering in his response to her strange request. He may have felt frustrated with the decision of her father that he felt was made recklessly, against the best interests of the children.

She stood there quietly, politely waiting, not agreeing with him, on the one hand, but not wanting to hurt or offend the good man, on the other. Of course they were very grateful to him for all his help...

Left with no other choice, the OSE activist acquiesced.

Two days passed, and Leah, Yankel and Naftoli were back and, mission accomplished, Sarah returned home with the children.

To this day it is a mystery what made Chaim Yair realize that the days of Château de Masgelier were numbered. Could it be that the establishment of the General Commissariat for Jewish Affairs in the beginning of 1941 was that final straw? Clearly, the Vichy regime was revving up toward mass incarceration and deportation of the Jews, which would come to a full display only a few months later, in June 1942, in the infamous Vel' d'Hiv roundup of over thirteen thousand Jews in Paris. But could it also be that events closer to home, of locals turning on the Jews, served him a cautionary sign? Maybe somehow the news of an incident that took place in Chaumont, a village fifty miles away from Château de Masgelier, reached him? The newly appointed priest of Chaumont denounced the Jewish children hiding there, which prompted their hasty escape. Maybe that was the last straw that made Chaim Yair decide that their time there was up?

In fact, many of the educators at Château de Masgelier had been apprehended by the Germans and either deported to Drancy, like Dr. Jean Cogan, Marcel Geisner, and Ignace Giblin, and from there continued to Auschwitz, or were executed on the spot, like Dr. Moise Blumenstock and his wife Gertrude. It was only a question of time until Château de Masgelier would be discovered and raided, Chaim Yair must have concluded.

The Château de Masgelier continued as a safe house for another two years, and then, in May of 1944, the OSE arrived to the same conclusion, that it was the time to flee. The persecution was already in full swing, and at the very last moment, in a daring operation, the children were taken in small groups to train stations in the area and dispersed to hide among the Christian families. But these children never found their way back to the Jewish nation.

Chaim Yair, it appears, decided to preempt these events. In the eye of the storm, the Weinstein family was together again.

*

Several months later, Sarah went with Miriam once again to search for food, going door to door, begging to buy whatever scraps of food the villagers were willing to sell.

They traveled further and further, taking a bus several hours away from their village. Miriam and Sarah chatted with each other in French, as the miles of mountains rolled by them.

An elderly man sitting near them on the bus interrupted their conversation. "I hear you talking French," he said. "But you're not from here, I can tell. Are you from the north? Alsace? Brittany? No, it's still different. Where are you from?"

Was it an attempt to pass the time? Was this the curiosity of a countryman who hadn't met many people from foreign places? Was he simply drawn to strike up a conversation with two attractive young girls? Was he speaking to them because people's hearts tend to open up on long roads, as if knowing that probably one won't ever meet that person again allows one's tongue to run loose?

Whatever the reason was for him initiating a conversation, it was one of those fateful encounters that would change everything for them, and once again save the family's life.

"We are from Antwerp," Sarah said. "We are refugees." She found the words popping out of her mouth, as though compelled by a hidden force.

"But why did you need to leave Antwerp? Is it any different than here?"

"We escaped when the bombing began. Our house was hit and we had nowhere to go, so we kept on going south." Sarah was good at giving very quick answers. Telling feasible stories, being talkative and open, sounded more credible, so that he wouldn't grow suspicious of a person who refused to say anything.

But she made sure not to mention their ethnicity, and the true reason for their escape. It was too risky, and too dangerous to reveal this to him. Without a star affixed to their clothing, there was nothing to make him realize they were Jewish.

"So where are you heading now?"

"To look for food," Miriam said simply. "There is no food in our village."

Just to make conversation she added, "Maybe you know where we can find food?"

Sarah and Miriam seemed to have touched something inside this old simple man. His face, lined with age, had an expression of openness and compassionate curiosity. His strong sinewy hands with skin darkened by years spent under the sun, told a story of hard work on his land. Wearing tattered, patched clothing was clear evidence that war was the biggest enemy of an honest man barely scraping together a living off his land.

"You know what? I do know a place. I can help you. My wife died recently and my house is empty. I just moved somewhere else. You can stay in my house rent free and there is plenty of food in my village. If you want, come with me and I'll show it to you. If you like it, stay there."

And just like that, they had a place to go, and a source of food.

Did he understand more than he was prepared to show? Did he realize that they were refugees of a very particular kind, the ones that didn't simply flee the ravages of war, but who had to run for their lives, fugitives on the entire continent? If he did, he didn't reveal this to them and they wouldn't know.

He explained to them how to find his home and Sarah and Miriam felt like they were in the midst of a magical moment. Could this really be happening? Why was he moved to do this? To give his home to strangers that he just met on the bus!

Without even saying his name or asking them theirs, when the bus neared his village, they disembarked and it seemed almost magical when they saw that it was small and rundown, more like a bungalow than a house, but it was a place where they could stay and survive. Two years of wandering taught them to know that life was never indulging them with luxury. They deeply appreciated this unexpected gift. Would their parents even believe them?

The old man showed them where he had left several bins full of root vegetables and said, "Please help yourselves. It's all yours."

When he left them there, Miriam and Sarah cleaned the dusty house, scrubbing down every surface, opening the windows to let in fresh air, to get ready for their family's arrival. Then they ventured into the village and managed to find a few straw mattresses and a stove to heat the house and cook food.

The village of Nantes-en-Ratier, two hundred miles northeast of Montpellier, and near Saint-Martin-de-la-Cluze, delivered as promised. There was plenty of corn, potatoes and beets available. A butcher and a baker also lived there in the village. Though it was a modest-sized place, it was completely self-sufficient. Amazed, they filled up their sacks and returned home triumphant, bursting to tell their family of this new development.

They knew that the food they were bringing was worth more than its weight in gold. Their parents could give a sack of potatoes, onions and chestnuts to the village doctor as a way of paying him for treating their mother. He had come so many times to make house visits, even though he knew they couldn't pay him.

Their mother was often sick, and now, with the stress of the fear of impending doom and having to flee before it was too late, their mother was ill again. Adversity was draining her of all energy, every drastic change rattled her terribly. Their mother was so sick that she needed to be admitted to the hospital in Montpellier.

Instinctively, their father Chaim Yair felt compelled by the urgency to move quickly.

"Malka, I've decided that I will take the children and go on ahead. I need you to stay in the city and visit your mother daily. You will wrap up your studies at the ORT school, Mama will be discharged from the hospital, and then you will both come join us."

But Malka no longer felt safe sleeping at the place where she had been boarding, at the old woman's house. She too felt like something significant had changed, and impending doom was in the air.

☙

The Vichy government no longer even had a facade of a self-governing entity. They were overrun by Nazi Germany, with the German High Command strategically positioned in the city of Vichy to command all the governmental business. Even though Marshal Phillipe Petain's government of Vichy France was officially a sovereign state, and French and German affairs were kept separate, to the point that foreign governments viewed Vichy France as a genuinely independent country, internally it no longer had any semblance of self-rule. They were simply puppets commanded by the German forces. Pressure was increasing to round up Jews and deport them.

But it was not just the pressure from the Germans. As historians have concluded, without the willing cooperation of the government of France, the Germans would not have had the necessary information about the French Jews to easily identify and deport them. French Jews were mostly assimilated and didn't have a distinct appearance. They looked just like their non-Jewish neighbors and easily blended into the general population, which did not make it so easy for a German to discern them among the ethnic French.

Also, embroiled in such massive military operations on so many fronts, from Northern and Western Europe all the way across the continent and deep into the steppes of Eastern parts of Russia and North Africa, the Germans lacked the manpower to identify and detain tens of thousands of people all across the country. Without the expertise and the resources of special police task force Commissariat Général aux Questions Juives, the Germans would not have been able to launch a nationwide operation against the Jews of France.

Historical documents and testimonies of former SS officers during trials prove beyond a doubt that the French were not victims in this regard, as they liked to portray themselves. Vichy authorities were very much willing, even enthusiastic, to enforce on their own accord the racial cleansing policies against the Jews. They even went beyond what was required of them by the Germans.

In a telegram that René Bousquet, secretary-general to the Vichy National Police, sent to all the Prefects overseeing the operation, he demanded to detain and deport not only foreign-born adults of Jewish origin, as the Germans ordered, but also children whose only crime was to be born Jewish.

Probably the single most damning testimony of the genocidal intent of French Vichy, proving that it was not isolated incidents led by local authorities that were acting on their own whim, but that it originated at the very top of the echelons of power, was a document that was unearthed only recently.

A draft of the original Statute on Jews, that vehemently anti-Semitic legislation passed by the French government in October, 1940, after defeat by the Nazis, reveals that Philippe Pétain, French national hero, with streets in France named after him to this day, completely redrafted the memo to make it even harsher and more wider-ranging. "The Statute on Jews was a Statute that was adopted without pressure from the Germans, without the request of the Germans: an indigenous Statute," said Serge Klarsfeld, Nazi hunter known for documenting the Holocaust in order to establish the record and to enable the prosecution of war criminals. "And now we have decisive evidence that it was the desire of Marshal Pétain himself."

Historical controversies of who is to blame aside, back in the beginning of 1942, the situation in France was becoming ominous. Fear of door to door searches was too overwhelming to bear.

❦

Malka was afraid to sleep in the apartment she shared with the elderly woman. She liked the woman and didn't want to leave her alone, but she was afraid of the consequences if she stayed. The woman's son and daughter lived in the city, so Malka knew that they could take care of their mother, while she wasn't a French citizen or registered in the city and she was at a great risk of deportation.

She needed to find a shelter for a few days, a neutral place where the police wouldn't be looking for her, until her mother recovered enough to leave the hospital and join the rest of the family in Nantes-en-Ratier. Desperation brought Malka to the doors of the city's convent.

"Please, may I have permission to sleep here for a few days?" she asked the nun who opened the doors.

To her great relief, the Mother Superior agreed. And once inside, she discovered that she wasn't the only Jewish girl to whom the nuns gave refuge. Another nine girls were hiding inside the walls of the convent.

In the morning after her first night there, Malka ventured out to go back to the ORT school to continue her studies. And after school she showed up at her job, as though everything was normal. She helped her teacher sew the dresses for her high heeled elite local clientele.

Later in life, Malka often wondered what happened to her kind teacher and employer, Mademoiselle Muller, a girl only a few years older than she. But her traces were lost in the storm of war.

A week later, Esther was finally discharged from the hospital and came to stay overnight with Malka at the convent. They made their last preparations before taking the long winding bus ride to Nantes-en-Ratier, the next morning, to their new home.

As they were about to go to sleep, Esther said to her daughter, "Let's go home first." Then she added, "I left some things there."

Malka didn't want to defy her mother but she was worried.

The next morning they walked to the station and took the bus back to their old village. When they were back in Prades-le-Lez, as they were about to go inside their old house that stood cold and empty, a neighbor saw them and exclaimed, "Oh, you're home?! The police came looking for you last week."

Pretending to innocently have a casual conversation, she was cautioning them. After some more hurried questions and answers, their talkative neighbor shared with them that the other Jewish family that had been hiding in the village, that included three generations of grandparents, parents and their children, had all been rounded up by the French police and deported to an internment camp.

From issuing laws discriminating people based on their race and occasionally going after individuals who they deemed undesirable, France had moved to the next, much darker phase in its history: wholesale operation of solving "the Jewish problem."

"Let's go," Malka said to her mother. "We must leave everything at once. We need to get out of here." Not willing to take the risk of waiting a few hours for the next bus out of the village, Malka and her mother simply started walking through the fields, away from the local police officers who would have recognized them on the spot, and most probably had them arrested, on the sweeping orders that came down from the very top of their command.

Malka and Esther had to run for their lives.

Even though the village was only two hundred miles from Prades-le-Lez, it took two days of travel by bus. Both communities were hidden in the midst of the countryside, which was a great advantage for anyone who tried to live a life under the radar. The downside of it was that no transportation was readily available, and the chaos of war made the travel even more difficult.

After several switchovers and stops and hours of traveling on foot, they finally arrived. Their family was together again, a tiny crew fighting their way through the tsunami of history.

Nantes-en-Ratier, a modest size community of less than four hundred inhabitants, was safely tucked away in the hills of the backcountry in southeast France, and living under the comparatively lax rule of Italian occupation. This was their new home, for now at least.

❦

Malka and Esther were shaken up by their close brush with danger. It was really close. So many things needed to happen in the exactly perfect way at the exactly perfect moment for them to keep their improbable streak of survival. If Chaim Yair didn't jump on that train, if he didn't call the children back from their safe haven, if Miriam and

Sarah hadn't met the old farmer who took a liking to them, if Chaim Yair didn't make a decision to leave immediately with the children without waiting for Esther's return from the hospital, they too would have been rounded up and disappeared like so many others. Call it serendipity or *hashgocha protis*, an invisible hand was leading them on their treacherous path, on a dangerously narrow bridge stretching across a deadly abyss, one step at a time.

But why? This was a question that they all asked themselves many times during the escape. What merit did they have to avoid the inevitable just in time? They were so vulnerable, looking so strikingly different. They stood out and drew unwanted attention, a big family with many little children. And yet, time and time again, they were saved, helped, led to the right place at exactly the right time…

CHAPTER TEN

# A Tiny Light in Colombière

They settled into their new home in the village of only a few dozen families, kind villagers who respected their privacy. Or put more precisely, the locals made a conscious effort to turn a blind eye. The very survival of the Weinstein's depended on the fact that this closely knit community, comprised of a handful of families living there for generations, would keep their affairs to themselves, and not go to the authorities to tell about an odd-looking family with an unusual amount of children that came from nowhere.

It was an open secret who the Weinstein's were and who they were hiding from. Unlike their stay at Montesquieu two years earlier, the times were very different, and the attitude of the authorities against the Jews had turned considerably worse. From confusion and general animosity, it crystallized into a hardened policy of open, unabashed persecution. As Petain publicly said, "Every Jew must be denounced," and many French people did indeed follow the call of their national hero and president.

But the inhabitants of the Nantes-en-Ratier deliberately, courageously, looked away. They were simple rural folks who knew how to keep secrets, and this offered the only chance the Weinstein family had to survive.

They all lived in one big room with a large stove, similar to the way people lived in the villages many centuries before. This was a rudimentary arrangement which turned out to be very practical for them. During the bitter cold of the winter, heating more than one room would have been an unaffordable luxury.

Esther had never learned French, but the older girls spoke it fluently.

Malka would often talk to the neighbors. "Why do you never buy meat?" one of them asked.

"We don't have enough money," she replied.

"Oh. That's a shame. It's so good and one animal can give you enough meat for a long time."

But even without meat, there was food. They could buy steaming milk straight from the cow; a curd of cheese made in a shed, and freshly baked bread straight from the oven. They no longer had food coupons, but the UJA had given the family a stipend, enough to buy the basic necessities that helped keep them alive.

For ten months they enjoyed a life of comparative serenity, precarious and fragile as it was.

Chaim Yair stayed indoors most of the time. The village, despite its isolated location, wasn't fully immune to police raids. Once Chaim Yair was alerted by the neighbors, just in time, that the gendarmes were about to swarm in searching for hiding *indésirables*.

He jumped out of the back window and fled to the woods. He waited there for the evening to descend, hiding behind the trees. Only when he saw the gendarmes wrap up the operation, climb into their navy blue Citroën police vans known as "Fourgonettes," and drive away, their round headlights piercing the night and illuminating the road one after the other, did he know that the search was over, and he could sneak back into the house.

Sometime in 1943, Chaim Yair received a postcard from his family. How they found his address and how it was even delivered to them, with their clearly foreign name written in plain sight, without the post office officials alerting the *Commissariat Général Aux Questions Juives*, they never found out.

But Malka remembers the look on her father's face as he dropped the postcard on the table and tore his shirt. The postcard, dated six days prior, notified him that his father Moshe Aryeh had passed away. Chaim Yair had one day left to sit *shivah*.

She remembered a similar moment back in Antwerp. The telegram had arrived on March 6, 1939, *Shushan Purim* that year, with the news that her grandmother, her father's mother Faiga Mirel had died, and that her father should say *kaddish*.

Malka was struck by a strange feeling she didn't even dare to think all the way through, let alone put into words, an apprehension of sorts that swirled around unarticulated. Who is the luckier one? Those who died before the war, who didn't have to be on the run anymore, to fear for their lives, to suffer the excruciating torture in those camps she'd heard about, or the ones who endured this travesty, hanging on to that elusive hope of the slightest chance of survival?

She kept thinking, some will eventually bear the unbearable and come out of the Holocaust alive, but so many won't. They will perish after all, having endured all the travails and the torment but still unable to outwit their fate. As King Solomon succinctly said, "I praised the dead that are already dead more than the living that are yet alive" (Ecclesiastes 4:2).

Begging for food for her family from the Italian soldiers that were quartered in the village, Miriam would contemplate on this age-old dilemma, shivering in the cold, her eyes downcast from humiliation. Will they make it? Will she make it, after all?

The searches became more focused and persistent. Gendarmerie would come into Nantes-en-Ratier repeatedly, clearly searching for someone. Apparently they acted on specific intelligence tips. Every time the police would sweep in, the community, a serene place where nothing ever happened, was rattled to the core.

One of the neighbors told the Weinstein's that a rumor had it that Chaim Yair, standing out because of his beard, was glimpsed by someone from outside the village who happened to be there on a random visit, and the gossip spread and reached the local authorities. It became clear by the day that the gendarmerie, combing through the village and questioning the inhabitants, would eventually lay their hands on the Weinstein's.

Their time at Nantes-en-Ratier, a hospitable hamlet lost in the backcountry of southeastern France, came to an end. Again, they were on the move, searching for a safe haven.

But now, this time they made a decision they had always tried to avoid. They decided it was safer to split apart. Chaim Yair was now a wanted fugitive and he needed to take extra care to stay in hiding. He would disappear, find himself a hideout at an undisclosed location, and the rest of the family would find another place, where they could live quietly, without drawing too much attention.

Just like any other family with a father away at war, they would do their best to blend in and stay low. For Chaim Yair it also would be much easier to be on his own. It would require less effort from him to do what it takes to survive with the bare minimum, something impossible to do with a large family with small children. And he would be more mobile in case of danger.

They found a place to stay, about forty miles north of Nantes-en-Ratier, in Colombière, a puny hamlet, with merely half a dozen derelict houses on top of a mountain overlooking Montaud, with another small community of two hundred residents in a valley underneath.

Located merely fifteen miles northwest of Grenoble, it had only two narrow access roads winding in the mountains. Ever since the Middle Ages this place was practically isolated from the outside world, hidden on the eastern slopes of Vercors mountain range at the heart of what is known today as the Auvergne-Rhône-Alpes region. It remained barely accessible all the same.

In Colombière, Esther was alone with the children again. The only difference was that Sarah, Miriam and Malka were fully grown young women, capable of taking care of the family, and of their mother.

There was one more difference. Esther was expecting a new child.

In March of 1943, Chaim Yair was hiding in undisclosed locations, always on the move, doing all he could to stay clear of his family. Should he be apprehended by the special police force of the *Commissariat Général aux Questions Juives*, they wouldn't be able to trace his wife and children down. Likewise, if they were to be questioned by the authorities as to his whereabouts, they also wouldn't, by any chance, by a slip of a tongue of one of the small ones, divulge his location, since they didn't know it.

As painful as it was for him to leave his family without him, knowing how heartbroken Esther was by his absence, he comforted himself by the thought that he wasn't deserting his family but quite the opposite. He was doing what our forefather Yaacov did: splitting his family into two camps and staying behind to fight the angel of darkness, in an effort to spare as many as he could of the people he loved the most.

With her baby's due date coming close, Esther made arrangements with a midwife from Montaud, about a mile and a half down the road in the valley, to come as soon as she went into labor. On one of those frosty nights in the mountains, when winter was in the air and remainders of snow turned into sleet, melting away under a bone-chilling drizzle with sudden gusts of wind blowing from the mountains, Esther went into labor.

Miriam and Malka walked through the drizzle, occasionally skidding on the sleet, turning their backs to violent bursts of frost blowing into their faces on that freezing cold wintry night.

A walk that would usually take no more than thirty-five minutes lasted for over an hour as they made their slow descent, with every step a struggle through the elements.

At last, they knocked on the midwife's door and waited and knocked again, until she came to answer it.

She clearly was not interested in braving the weather and climbing two hundred feet up the mountain.

"I'm sure she has plenty of time," the midwife said dismissively. Her warm cozy bedroom, with a bed covered by a puffy feather blanket and embers glowing in a hearth, was beckoning.

"Please," Malka begged. "My mother is not young. You have to come. You can't leave her alone to have this baby."

After a great deal of wrangling, the midwife begrudgingly acquiesced. She wrapped herself in extra layers of clothing and then they stepped out into the biting cold to begin the climb up the mountain to Colombière. Gusts of wind blew powerfully against them, bursts of heavy rain soaked them, and fog enveloped the mountain, making the path under the feet difficult to see. With every step the girls were praying that the midwife wouldn't have a change of heart and turn back. The way up took even much longer than the descent.

As they were approaching the first houses of Colombière, hints of navy blue hue began to stretch across the far edges of the horizon.

They were gone for so long that when they finally returned, their mother was lying in a room lit only with the barely glowing ashes in the stove that had already started cooling off. They hurried to bring in more wood from the back of the shed to stoke the fire.

While they were busy trying to heat up the room, the midwife gave Esther a cursory check and announced, "Too early," and without giving the girls any chance to protest, she walked out the door.

Malka and Miriam felt lost. They couldn't take any more chances arguing with her and risk getting her frustrated even more than she already was. The very survival of their entire family depended on her willingness to keep their identity secret.

As the labor progressed, the contractions became more intense. Esther had already given birth to nine children, and was more than prepared for the labor pains awaiting her that would bring her new baby into the world. She knew full well to breathe into contractions, and ease into the challenge of labor.

But she sensed that this was different. Never before were the pains so unbearable. Even Naftoli, sleeping in another room, who never woke up even when people were talking loudly right next to his bed, woke up in fright, startled by his mother's anguished cries, as she was gasping in agony.

Homebirth was a normal event. It was only on rare occasions that a woman would check herself into a hospital to give birth. The older girls, who had been home during the births of their younger siblings, knew this was different and knew that they must get help for their mother immediately. Malka rushed across the street and banged on the door of their neighbor, an older woman who they knew had her share of life challenges.

When she opened her door, Malka begged, "Please, please help us! Something is wrong! Our mother is in danger!" She kindly dashed back with Malka, but she really had no idea what she could do.

Malka raced back out and ran to another neighbor, an older man who had a bicycle. "Please," she pleaded with tears of desperation in her eyes. "My mother is having a baby. She is dying. We need a doctor immediately. Please get us a doctor."

The old man did not hesitate, despite the frigid weather. He hopped on his bicycle and took off immediately down the road to Montaud, where he knew a doctor lived. Fortunately, the doctor was home, was not attending another emergency in some other hamlet in the area and was willing to come.

By the time he arrived in his buggy and horse, Esther had already given birth to a boy, assisted only by the neighbor from across the street. The first thing he saw when he entered the room was that the bed was soaked with blood. Esther was bleeding profusely, barely hanging on to life.

Experienced with emergencies like this, he asked the girls to bring him boiled water to sterilize his equipment, and to get as many clean towels as they could find. He put a bowl of warm water on a bench next to him and started a field surgery, stitching the many tears that were caused by the difficult birth.

He succeeded in stopping the excessive bleeding and saved Esther's life. If he had arrived just a few minutes later, the outcome would have been tragically different.

The doctor instructed the girls how to care for their mother during her recovery.

"It is very important," he warned them, "that your mother rests in bed for a long time to heal and recuperate. She should not lift anything heavy for at least six weeks. Otherwise the sutures might open and she will start bleeding again. If the wounds open again, the situation could become much more dangerous because repairing the tissue will be more complicated, if at all possible," was his stern warning.

He softened a bit and offered a bit of medical explanation. "Your mother is not young. The hardships she has faced and poor nutrition compromised her health, and on top of it she has already had many births." He didn't sound very approving of this particular detail, but he stayed on the topic. "Because of all of this, her body will need more time to recover. So be prepared to be patient. It is going to be a long convalescence."

❦

Just a few days after the birth, while Miriam and Malka were home alone with their mother and their younger siblings had ventured out to enjoy the warm beautiful weather, there was a loud knock on the door.

Malka opened the door and a tall, burly policeman stepped right in, without asking permission. His partner stayed outside to guard the door and keep an eye on the street.

"Come with us," the policeman said brusquely to the girls. He didn't even care to glance at Esther, still weak from the birth, sitting in bed with a baby in her arms.

Malka and Miriam turned pale.

"Please," Malka begged in a trembling voice, feeling everything crashing down on her, fearing that the worst had come upon them. "My mother is very ill. The doctor said she shouldn't get out of bed."

"She can stay," he retorted. "You two, you and your sister, come with us." "But she needs our help. We can't leave her alone," Malka was in tears, paralyzed with terror.

He stared back unmoved, sizing her up with his watery eyes full of gleeful contempt, when the other policeman stepped in and said, "Leave them alone. Let's move."

And just like that, they were gone, leaving the girls and Esther confused, terrified, shaken to their core, wondering if it was only a question of time, maybe hours, until an entire squad of gendarmerie would descend on their shack, scoop them all up and haul them away.

Incredibly, they will never know why, no one returned.

❦

Historically, French police had a patchy history during World War Two. After the surrender of France, a majority of file and rank policemen, many of whom hailed from the military, followed their national hero

Marshal Philippe Pétain, the Head of Vichy regime, welcoming the collaboration with the Germans. But gradually the resentment in the police ranks grew. The French felt they were fighting a war that was not theirs, for causes they grew more and more disenfranchised with. More and more cases of dissent or outright defiance became a new norm, and the Germans had a hard time demanding persecution of those dissenters, as this would have undermined the good will of the French public.

When the Jews of Paris were rounded up in mid-July of 1942, the French were shocked. They witnessed thousands of men, women and children, from babies to the frail elderly, herded into the big Vélodrome d'Hiver stadium, like cattle, and from there marched to a train station and loaded on trains. Everyone knew that these people who lived by their side their entire lives, who shopped at the same stores and worked in the same jobs and frequented the same cafes, their doctors and lawyers, their shopkeepers and tailors, were sent to Drancy, and from there to Auschwitz. All of a sudden, the French woke up and saw their own complicity, in its full, disgraceful display. They were horrified.

Following the public outrage, the Mayor of Paris even told the German High Command, "Don't ask for our Jews anymore." This obviously drew the ire of the Nazis, but they were helpless to do anything about it. Stretched thin on all fronts, they lacked the manpower and the resources to summon full control of the city, and had to swallow the humiliation. From that moment on, the regular French police were reduced to a peripheral role of securing the perimeter during the aktion, guarding public buildings and patrolling train stations.

The visit that the two policemen paid the Weinstein's in the puny hamlet of Colombière may have been no more than a prank. Likely, it was a cruel joke of two bored cops used to abuse of power, for the sheer fun of watching the hunted down Jews shake in terror. It could be that these two crass men were even hoping that in those days of reign of terror and compromised morality, they could extort some personal favors from these two pretty, young girls, if only they made it clear that their very survival depended on them.

Years later, when Malka remembered that terrifying incident, those moments of dread and uncertainty, it would still hit her in the gut, that feeling of no control, being at the mercy of people she knew had too much power and too little integrity to match it, flailing on a thin thread that could break at any moment.

Despite the traumatic birth, the baby was healthy and his weight was within normal range. But he couldn't have a *bris* on the eighth day. Under the persecution of the Nazis, with everyone either on the run or hiding or already ensnared in internment camps, it was almost impossible to find a *mohel*, let alone bring him out of hiding and have him travel across enemy territory, putting his life in danger, to do the *bris*. It took Chaim Yair, who was communicating with his family from a safe distance, a full four months to find a *mohel* he could trust and who would trust him, a devout man he knew back from the old days, from Antwerp.

The *mohel* arrived in their home and was preparing the baby for the *bris*, when suddenly, unexpectedly, their father walked into the room, as if he had materialized out of thin air.

Grateful and amazed that they were all together, Chaim Yair was the *sandek*.

Their baby was named Meir, after Esther's grandfather, her father's father, a name that in Hebrew means illuminating light. They hoped and prayed that he would be a source of light in a dark world and by the time he would grow up, the world would have emerged from the darkness it was immersed in.

In the months before their baby was born, Esther had dreamed of her mother. "You will have a boy," her mother said. "And his name will be Meir." Esther had dismissed the dream back then, but here she was holding her son named Meir.

As soon as the *bris* was over, Chaim Yair kissed all his children and slipped back into the woods of the Vercors Mountains surrounding Colombière. Where did he go? They had no clue. They realized only that he was hiding somewhere near, and that he was still taking care of them, even from afar. He lived in the shadows, to protect them and himself, and now he had dissolved back into obscurity again.

*Chaim Yair Weinstein, Antwerp, Belgium, before World War II*

*Esther Weinstein, circa 1949*

*The Weinstein family in Montesquieu, France, 1940
Front row (l–r): Avraham Duvid, Gitele, Yankel, Leah, Berel,
Naftoli Back row (l–r): Malka, Esther, Chaim Yair, Sarah, Miriam*

*Gurs labor camp, France. Rabbi Chaim Yair Weinstein miraculously escaped from this concentration camp in 1940*

*Camp d'Agde, France, where the family was held from 1940 to 1941, when they were released due to influence of Madame Aron Lourié*

USNS Henry Gibbins, the ship that transported the refugees to safety in America

Yankel and Leah Weinstein aboard the USNS Henry Gibbins, 1944

Yankel Weinstein in a striped shirt
aboard the USNS Henry Gibbins, 1941

Jacques and Hélène Bloch and the teachers at the Château du Masgelier, ca. 1941–1943

Château du Masgelier, France, the orphanage where the OSE hid the Weinstein children in 1941

Children helped plant potatoes at the Château du Masgelier.

The Weinstein children in Oswego, New York, eating their first American ice cream, 1944
Top (l–r): Miriam and Malka. Bottom (l–r): Naftali, Leah, Yankel and Berel

The Weinstein family (l–r): Naftoli, Yankel, Miriam, Leah, Malka, and Berel, circa 1951

*Jacqui Sussholz's wedding: (l–r):* Danny
Sussholz, Jacqui Sussholz, Dovid Sussholz,
Sarah Sussholz, Miriam Newman, Belgium

*Esther Weinstein with Sarah
Sussholz, Antwerp, Belgium, 1960*

*Dovid Sussholz (left) at his son
Moshe's wedding, Belgium, 1976*

*Sarah Sussholz and Miriam
Newman, Belgium, 1976*

*Malka Weinstein's wedding portrait, Brooklyn, New York, 1949*

*Malka Weinstein Greenzweig (in white outfit) and Sherry Weinstein*

*Miriam Weinstein and Avraham Newman, on their wedding day, June 1953*

*The Weinstein family at Miriam Weinstein and Avraham Newman's wedding, June 1953
Front row (l–r), Miriam Weinstein and Avraham Neuman, Esther Weinstein
Back row (l–r): Mordechai Yoel and Malka Greenzweig; Gitel, Leah,
Yaakov, Avraham Duvid, Berel, Naftoli, and Meir Weinstein.*

*The extended Weinstein and Newman families at Miriam Weinstein and Avraham Newman's wedding, June 1953.*
*Front row (l–r) Mordechai Yoel and Malka Greenzweig, Miriam, Avraham, Esther, Elsie, Meir*
*Back row (l–r) Naftoli, Riftcha, Berel, Beri Gutman, Gitel, Leah, Mrs. Weiner, Mrs. Tauber, Yisroel Weiner, Yaakov, Dovid.*
*(Girls sitting on floor unknown)*

*Miriam Newman with two of her children.*

*Miriam Newman*

*The Newman family: (l–r): Mechel Newman, Raizy Katz (Newman), Miriam Newman, Avraham Newman, Shmiel Newman*

*Berel Weinstein, 1948*

*The Nitra Yeshiva, Berel Weinstein (third from right) next to Rabbi Michoel Ber Weissmandel and Rabbi Eliezer Silver (center), 1948*

*Berel Weinstein, New York, 1964*

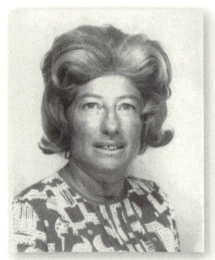

Leah Weinstein Gottfried

Leah Weinstein Gottfried

Leah Weinstein with her husband, Shloime Gottfried, and children, Israel

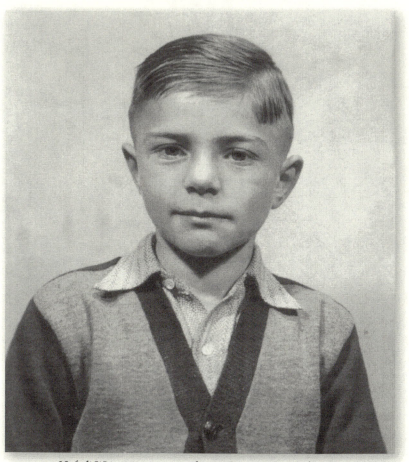
*Naftali Weinstein as a young boy in Oswego, New York, 1944*

*Esther Weinstein with her new daughter-in-law Sherry, aka Chaya Golda, December 17, 1963, Broadway Central Hotel in New York City.*

*Sarah Sussholz, Malka Weinstein Greenzweig, Miriam Weinstein Newman, and Sherry Weinstein at Naftali and Sherry's wedding, December 17, 1963*

Naftali and Sherry Weinstein's wedding, Broadway Central Hotel, New York, New York, December 17, 1963.
Back row (l–r): Malka Greenzweig, Sarah Sussholz, Miriam Newman Esther Weinstein, Sherry Weinstein, Naftali Weinstein, Yankel Weinstein, Dovid Sussholz, Mordechai Yoel Greenzweig, Meyer Weinstein, Avraham Duvid Weinstein, Avraham Newman
Front row (l–r): Raizy Neuman, Goldy Greenzweig, Mechel Neuman, Hershy Greenzweig, Shmiel Neuman, Shulem Greenzweig

*Naftoli Weinstein at the engagement of Raizy Newman to Favel Katz, Brooklyn, NY April 1974*

*Gitel Weinstein holding Raizy Newman, Catskill Mountains, summer 1955*

*Avraham Duvid Weinstein (center), Berel Weinstein (far right), others unknown, circa 1970.*

*Avraham Duvid Weinstein*

*Avraham Duvid Weinstein*

*Meir Weinstein as a child*

*Meir Weinstein as a child*

*Meir Weinstein at his bar mitzvah, 1956*

*The extended family at Meir and Brocha Weinstein's wedding, 1971
Back row (l–r) – Yankel Weinstein, Shulem Greenzweig, Mordechai Yoel Greenzweig, Dovid Sussholz, Avrohom Newman, Unknown, Naftali Weinstein, Shloime Weinstein, rest unknown.
Middle Row (l–r) Unknown, Sarah Sussholz, Malka Greenzweig, Mayer Weinstein, Bracha Weinstein, Sherry Weinstein, Miriam Newman, unknown.
Front row (l–r) Goldie Friedman, Raizy Katz, Shmiel Newman, Mechel Newman, Tzvi Hersh Greenzweig.*

*Esther Weinstein and Mayer, Switzerland, 1946*

*Esther Weinstein holding Mayer Weinstein. Others unknown*

*L-R Moshe Sussholz, Kela Sussholz, Esther Weinstein, Gittel Weinstein, Jacqui Sussholz, Antwerp, Belgium, circa 1947*

CHAPTER ELEVEN

# "Who, Being Loved, Is Poor?"

That horrific 1943, four endless years since the furnace of the Holocaust started spitting fire, when last hopes were dashed and the extermination of the Jews raged unabated all across Europe, there were an estimated 42,500 camps and ghettos devouring millions upon millions of human lives. That same year, Sarah was offered a *shidduch*.

The suggestion, surprising at first, came from an elderly man who lived in Grenoble, a major city since antiquity, at the foot of the French Alps, capital of the district of Isère, merely fifteen miles southeast of Colombière.

The old man met Sarah on one of her voyages in search of food. On that day, she and Miriam were scouting out in Grenoble. She saw him, a frail shell of a human being going through dumpsters for scraps of anything that would be remotely edible. She simply couldn't pass by.

She approached the poor man and asked him if he needed food, a typical thing Sarah would do. The little she had, she would share with others.

"What a question!" he said, unsteady on his feet, weak, an imperceptibly humorous smirk burrowing even deeper into his wrinkled, unshaven face. "Of course I do."

All they had was a few potatoes and a pinch of butter. Sarah thought for a moment to simply give the poor man two potatoes, but he appeared too weak to even prepare them. She was at a loss of what to do.

"I can give you the two potatoes. But do you have where to cook them?"

The man said, in faint hope, "I live nearby."

Sarah was resolute, "Let me help you with that."

They walked to the dingy rooms he called home. As Miriam watched her sister light up the stove, grind the potatoes, melt a tiny bit of butter and fry latkes for a stranger, she thought to herself, "I wish I was like her. But is it even practical to be like her?"

As it says, כל ישראל ערבים זה לזה – all the Jews are guarantors for each other. Sarah went out of her way to save from starvation the old man she didn't know. Then the chain of kindness continued, as he extended a helping hand to a Jew in danger. He opened up his modest home to a young man named Dovid Sussholz, who had escaped from Germany and was wanted by the Gestapo for his underground activity.

In those desperate days of widespread, ongoing destruction, many were so diminished that they could barely care for their own, hearts were numb, and turning a blind eye to the difficulties that others were facing, was the common way of coping. Being a generous person and sharing with others the dismally little one had demanded a great deal of moral virtue.

Sarah exhibited just that, and the old man from Grenoble knew that there was something very special about her.

After getting to know this young man Dovid who was now staying in his home, he decided to set Dovid up with the kind girl who had fed him.

"You're alone," he said to Dovid. "And I know a girl who is religious just like you."

On her occasional trips to Grenoble, Sarah visited the old man and she met Dovid there.

Life was hard and no one knew if they would live to see another day and each day felt like it was the last. Everyone was living on edge, and feelings were razor sharp. The emotional soundtrack of those harrowing days was one of danger, of living with fear, bereavement, and the numbing pain of loss. Who could think of marriage during these times full of despair?

And yet, there also was the desperate, the impossible, the fragile hope, living with an unquenched desire to celebrate one more day, to love, to be loved, even at the very darkest hour. Only this intense will to go on living, against all odds, this courage gave them the strength to defy death, to not fall into the deepest pit of despondency, to not surrender to the monster that came after their souls.

Entrusting your heart to someone you could lose at any moment was sheer madness. But the desire to belong, to love and be loved in the midst of a brutal, bleeding world where millions were killing millions, was the only thing that made sense to live for.

In the abyss of despair, Dovid and Sarah found each other.

It didn't take long before Dovid and Sarah traveled to meet her father. They found him in St. Gervais, another tiny community of three hundred and forty inhabitants, merely ten miles down the winding mountainous road from Colombière, squeezed between the Isère River and Vercors Massif, an auxiliary of the French Alps.

In the seventeenth century, St. Gervais was famous for its ore and the foundry where cannons were cast and shipped down the river to the arsenal of the Royal Navy in the coastal city and naval port of Toulon. The cannons manufactured in St. Gervais, unparalleled in their quality, all had a famous motto engraved on their barrels, "*Ultima ratio regum*," – "the last reason of kings."

Four hundred years later, in 1943, cannons, the weapon of madmen and dictators, were again tearing the world apart. During World War Two, St. Gervais was a minuscule community, and a handful of Jews were hiding there. Chaim Yair was among them.

Dovid Sussholz asked Chaim Yair for a blessing to marry his daughter. Chaim Yair knew very little about the young man. He knew only that he came from a very religious family, originally from Germany, that he had gone to the prestigious Etz Chaim *yeshivah* in Heide, a village fifteen miles north of Antwerp. The *yeshivah* was established by Rabbi Shraga Feivel Shapiro in 1931 and renowned for being the first *yeshivah* in Belgium.

Chaim Yair could also sense his future son-in-law's laid back and agreeable demeanor, which well complemented Sarah's strong and independent character. He blessed the young couple that they should merit to build a beautiful Jewish home with a strong foundation and bear fruit for many years to come. In those harrowing days, this was not a trivial blessing.

When Chaim Yair told his good friend Mr. Paissochowitz the good news that his daughter was engaged, of course Mr. Passochowitz asked, "So who's the boy?"

"His name is Dovid Sussholz."

"Sussholz?! One of the Sussholz brothers!? He is wanted by the Gestapo! There are *Wanted, Dovid Sussholz* leaflets circulating everywhere. Your whole family is in mortal danger if your daughter marries him," he declared passionately.

"He must be an amazing boy, I have nothing against him, but if the Gestapo is in hot pursuit after him, then your family will also be accused of collaboration if you have any connection with him. Even if you are in hiding, so the gendarmerie can't find you, that doesn't mean you or your family are safe. No Italians will save this boy – and your family – from them."

According to a tenuous arrangement between the Italian Occupation Forces and German High Command, neither the German Gestapo nor the French Commissariat Général Aux Questions Juives, the General Commissariat for the Jewish Affairs, would go after regular people living under the Italian military rule. But there was a caveat. If that person was accused of a specific "crime," then the Italians had to step down, and the Gestapo or the French special task force were granted the authority to pursue their target and prosecute them or whoever was associated with their victim.

Dovid's brother Leo, several years older than him, had many contacts in the Resistance, the underground movement that fought the Nazis. They would sabotage German armed forces, detonate rail tracks and thus stop movement of military equipment and personnel. Among other ventures, they set up a sophisticated network of forging documents and a sprawling smuggling network, helping tens of thousands of Jews escape to unoccupied parts of France, Switzerland and Spain. One of Leo Sussholz's contacts stole original stamps from the Gestapo, which made it possible to forge different documents, including even the IDs of the German military personnel.

Leo helped smuggle people over the harsh terrain of the Pyrenees Mountains, and into Spain. Even though Franco, the fascist dictator of Spain, signed a pact with Germany during World War Two, Spain remained a non-belligerent country, meaning that it didn't participate in war on either side. Just like Switzerland, Spanish neutrality made sure it wouldn't be invaded either by the Axis or by the Allies.

In the summer of 1942, when Germany started deporting Jews to extermination camps, many Jewish refugees crossed illegally into Catalonia, the northern region of Spain.

The escape routes across the Pyrenees passed through the most inhospitable areas of the region, as these were the ones least watched by German patrols. To avoid being detected, the fugitives, many of whom traveled in the only clothing and shoes they had, unsuitable for the high mountains, had to walk at night, stumbling their way through the treacherous trails, shivering in the freezing cold of high altitudes. They walked almost at a crawl, because the groups were mostly comprised of children, older and sick people, all of them suffering from malnutrition.

If they were spotted by gendarmerie or Nazis, they were sent directly to the extermination camps. Even when they arrived at the first post of Spain's Civil Guard, they were not yet free. First, they were locked up in Sort prison, in pitiful conditions. And some, if they were unlucky, were sent back to France, from where they were sent to the camps, facing almost certain death.

When the Allies became aware of the Spanish policies toward the refugees, they warned Franco's government that the fate of these refugees would have a major impact on Allied policy toward Spain. In other words, returning the refugees to the hands of the Nazis and thus condemning them to a death would be viewed as an act of war, and the Allies would attack Spain.

Fearing retribution, Spain announced in April 1943 that it would admit refugees, as long as some other party would provide for their care and the refugees would leave the country as fast as they could. The mechanism was promptly set up, and the refugees were mainly provided for by the Joint Distribution Committee in Spain. Now the Resistance network had a comparatively safe destination for all those people escaping the German killing machine. The operation of smuggling people from France to Spain kicked into high gear, and Leo Sussholz and his friend Richard were part of it, risking their lives on a daily basis.

Smuggling was a precarious business, and the day arrived when the Sussholzes were ready to smuggle themselves into France and save their own lives while it was still possible. Leo and his friend Richard put on the stolen uniform of a Nazi major. Dovid, dressed as their chauffeur, was wearing well-tailored civilian clothes with a swastika on the lapel of his jacket. Their sister Fraidel traveled in a disguise as their secretary. They looked like a regular military team traveling on official business. Were they to be stopped, they'd show their impeccably forged ID documents and be flagged through the check post, as they'd done so many times before.

Close to the border, the car broke down and Dovid managed to get it to a garage. They never discovered what aroused the mechanic's suspicion. Perhaps it was forbidden for a military car to go to a civilian garage. Perhaps the rank insignias on Leo and Richard's uniforms weren't one hundred percent in accordance with the rules. Whatever the case, two German officers approached them as they waited for their car to be repaired. "This is a border zone," they said. "Please show us your papers."

They glanced at their documents. "We need you to come to our command center," one of them said. Leo was asked to join one officer in his car, while one officer sat next to Dovid in their car and ordered him to drive to the center. The Germans meticulously went through the contents of their car once they arrived. The forgery and the incriminating supplies were promptly discovered.

They admitted they were Jews, but the Nazis initially didn't believe them. They never believed that Jews would be capable of such things. They were convinced they'd discovered a large spy network.

Nazi uniform stripped off of them, their hands tied behind their backs, Leo and Richard were savagely beaten, but Fraidel and Dovid were initially spared.

The Germans brought them to the Gestapo in Lyon where they were interrogated. At each interrogation Dovid had to introduce himself as "party member with such and such number but in reality the pig Jew Dovid Sussholz."

Leo was injured with a dagger during one of the interrogations and was sent to the hospital to recover from his wound.

In the prison, Richard and Dovid were put in a section called Montluc, infamous in Lyon for its interrogations. Once, when they were in the courtyard of the Montluc prison, a Gestapo man came and asked, "Who speaks German and is willing to work?" Richard and Dovid stepped forward. The Gestapo officer didn't know their background, otherwise he never would have offered them the opportunity.

Richard had told Dovid that if he ever got a chance to escape, he would do so. Dovid couldn't bear to leave his sister and brother behind. But when they were working in the warehouse, emptying it of wine, there came a moment of confusion, when the guards were busy drinking and he was faced with an excruciating decision. Any attempt to rescue the others would be doomed, and as painful as it was, he felt compelled to escape, make his way back to the town and alert countless others that their identities and whereabouts were soon to be extorted in torture. Even if Leo and Fraidel and Richard were going to die, he would not be able to save them. But he had to do all he could to save as many as possible.

Richard had managed to escape and hired a truck driver to bring them from southern France, all the way from the Pyrenees to the Auvergne-Rhône-Alpes region, a distance of almost five hundred miles. Dovid made his way to the relative safety of Grenoble where the elderly man had given him refuge. But now his name was on every wanted list of highly dangerous fugitives all across France, and a warrant for his arrest and hefty monetary compensation were put out for him.

This was the story of Dovid Sussholz that he told Chaim Yair. He was an unassuming, easy going young man with a bashful smile.

Shaken by this harrowing account, and though he was deeply impressed by this young man and saddened for the tragic losses he suffered, Chaim Yair felt he owed it to the safety of his family to postpone the engagement. As he voiced his doubts to the young couple, he was quite shocked by Sarah's reaction.

"Tatteh! How long do you think we should wait? Nothing has broken me before! Not the poverty, not the searching for food and begging people for it! Not the deportation, not the d'Agde camp and not even mother almost dying in labor before my eyes!!

"If we wait, how do you know we will even be alive then?"

She could not be comforted. The fear that had made him hesitate dissipated before his daughter's impassioned words that gave him the strength to change his mind. His daughter, so selfless, so giving, so brave, deserved her bright moment of happiness in the dark valley of tears. He realized that whatever danger they would be in, whatever was going to happen in their future, they would face it together.

Their wedding took place in St. Gervais, in the shadow of the beautiful French Alps, on a hot summer day in August of 1943. It was a small wedding, with barely a *minyan* present, with scraps of food and no music. They did not want to draw any attention to their celebration.

But their mother prepared for them a surprise, something unforgettable in those days of scarcity. Esther prepared a cheesecake.

"Oh, a cheesecake, a *kwarktaart*," the family exclaimed in great wonder. This was an unbelievable treat that made them feel like they were at a true feast. Everything tasted delicious in wartime, but the original Belgian cheesecake made of *quark*, with a crunchy crust made of spicy freshly baked *speculaas* biscuit at the bottom, reminded them of Antwerp.

Even with the famous Belgian chocolate that was usually on top replaced by the wild berries that the younger Weinstein's picked in the nearby forest, the *kwarktaart* reminded them of better times, offering a tiny taste of hope, a glimmer of faith that miracles are possible, just like love was possible.

The guests, destitute as they were, gave the newlyweds a spoon as a gift. Only those who've faced tragedy, who don't know if they will live to see the sunrise next morning, know what happiness is, how pure the joy can be.

Dovid and Sarah were very grateful and joyous to reach this momentous moment in their lives.

The next day they traveled up the road to Colombière, picked up the few possessions that Sarah had, stopped briefly at their matchmaker's house in Grenoble, and continued down the road on the western slopes of the Varcors Massif to Nantes-en-Ratier, the old community where the Weinstein's lived before.

Their old shack stood empty. More than half a year had passed since the Weinstein's fled the place. They hoped and prayed that no one was going to pay attention to a quiet couple that returned to take up residence there and live in modest simplicity.

CHAPTER TWELVE

# Passage in the Night

The Holocaust was raging in its unabated fury, but the Weinstein family, scattered across the tiny communities of a barely accessible region of Isère, enjoyed a temporary calm under the relative protection of the Italian occupation. Unbeknownst to them, they owed their survival to one man whose name they didn't even know, Cavalier Angelo Donati, a Jewish banker hailing from a very influential Jewish family from Modena in northern Italy.

Angelo Donati served as an ambassador of The Most Serene Republic of San Marino (a microstate surrounded by Italy) in Paris. He fled to the south of France right before the German invasion and settled in Nice, a port city in Côte d'Azur, in the French coastal area of the Mediterranean. There he went on to serve as a director of the Franco-Italian Bank.

When Nice came under Italian occupation in November of 1942, his position rendered him a great deal of influence with the Italian military and diplomatic corps, which he decided to put to good use rescuing the Jews all across the Italian occupied parts of France.

Thanks to Angelo Donati, the General Consul of Italy, Alberto Calisse, halted the deportation of the Jews in the Vichy Republic to concentration camps in Poland. The German authorities in Rome were so infuriated by this audacious interference that the Italian dictator Benito Mussolini was forced to create a Crown Office of Racial

Police in Nice, and assigned Inspector Guido Lospinoso to run it. After reporting to his new position, Inspector Lospinoso met with the most influential Italian in Nice, Angelo Donati, who successfully convinced him to effectively sabotage the very office he was heading.

When the Vichy Government ordered the Prefect of Nice, Marcel Ribière, to arrest all the foreign Jews in Côte d'Azur, no other than General Avarna di Gualtieri, Head of the Supreme Italian command in Vichy, influenced by Angelo Donati, declared any decisions against the Jews in the Italian occupation zone void, reasoning that "these decisions have to be taken only by Italian military occupation authorities."

Nevertheless, despite its comparatively benevolent role toward the Jews, Italy was an ally of Nazi Germany, and effectively a combatant enemy state against the Allies. At the same time as Dovid and Sarah were dating in Grenoble, the Allied Forces landed blows on Italy in quick succession. On July 10, they landed in Sicily, driving the Italian armed forces to a brink of collapse. A week later, on July 19, 1943, for the first time ever, Rome, a timeless symbol of Italian heritage, was raided by the Allied air force. Explosions rocked the entire area, sending plumes of ash and concrete and clouds of black smoke up in the azure blue skies of the Eternal City.

Merely five days later, on July 24, the Italian government voted no confidence in Benito Mussolini and asked the king of Italy, Victor Emmanuel III, to assume the constitutional powers and remove Mussolini from power. Mussolini ignored the move, thinking that no one could touch him. As Mussolini left his audience with the king, he was arrested by the Carabinieri Italian police, outside the royal palace.

Marshal Pietro Badoglio, the newly appointed Prime Minister of Italy, announced that he was continuing the war effort in alliance with Nazi Germany. He was buying time, staving off German retribution. In the meantime, he started negotiating an armistice with the Allies, which took him just over a month to sign, on September 3, 1943.

One month after Dovid and Sarah Sussholz celebrated their modest wedding, the Italian armistice with the Allies became a fait accompli, which prompted ferocious German retaliation. They attacked their former allies on every front where the Italian forces were positioned – in the South of France, in the Balkans, and in Italy proper. Italian forces, no match for a hardened German military machine, were quickly defeated and retreated from all the territories they occupied. Moreover, the entire northern and central part of the Italian peninsula, including Rome, was now overrun by German troops.

By the end of September, Germans pushed the Italian army out of the areas they occupied until then. They were free now to do as they wished. While fifty-two thousand Jews were rounded up and deported from France to Poland to inevitable death, on the southern Franco-Italian border, the Weinstein's, along with twenty-five thousand more Jews who were hiding in the shadows of Italian occupation, were desperately trying to cross the border, following the Italians. As the Italians retreated, endless transports with refugees followed them in lockstep, figuring it would be safer to take refuge in a country that was now affiliated with the Allies. Many large and small rescue and relief organizations joined efforts in gathering the Jews that were hiding all across southeast France to help lead their mass exodus.

Among them was the juggernaut Joint Distribution Committee that spent a staggering $70,235,876, equaling 1.26 billion US dollars today, to save the Jews in the Holocaust, to the OSE that saved children under German occupation, to Rue Amelot, a clandestine organization which ran a network of agents informing the Jews of impending roundups, arrests and deportations, to Delegazione Assistenza Emigranti Ebrei, or DELASEM, the Delegation for the Assistance of Jewish Immigrants, an umbrella organization based in Italy. All the rescue organizations directed the Jews from the region to converge on Modane, a community in the Savoie department on the Franco-Italian border, with a major train hub and a tunnel running under the Alps, connecting the two countries.

"Women and children on the buses, everyone else on the train," the organizers said.

Six months after birth, Esther was still weak. Malka wanted to come with her and help her mother care for baby Meir, three-year-old Avraham Duvid and five-year-old Gittele.

But she wasn't allowed on the bus.

"Only mothers with small children," they insisted.

The buses were more convenient and wouldn't make as many stops along the way, but there were only that many people that could fit in them. All the others had to take trains, packed beyond capacity, not very different from the other trains, taken at the very same time in a different location, to a whole different horrible destination...

The family separated. Esther went with the three smaller children and boarded the bus. Chaim Yair went on the train with the older ones and the newlyweds, Sarah and Dovid. The Weinstein's, with their forged papers claiming French citizenship, crossed the border into the German controlled Northern Italy. The Germans at the border, overwhelmed by chaos, had a hard time distinguishing between the Jews and the Italians who looked all the same to them. They didn't pay enough attention and waved them through. The Weinstein's crossed into Italy without incident.

A week later, the Allied Air Force destroyed Gare de Modane, the railway station, rendering the rail tracks useless.

The Jews made it just in time, or so they thought. Everyone believed that Italy, having aligned itself with the Allies, now came under the Allies' military control. They were tragically mistaken. Many Jews who raced across the border found themselves in the midst of a Nazi trap. The signposts moved together with them. Nazi Germany invaded northern Italy and rolled all the way down to Rome. The refugees were under German genocidal rule again, only now they were no longer protected by the Italian military. They were again under an imminent threat of deportation and extermination.

But neither the Weinstein's nor anyone else knew that. They thought they were riding out to safety.

Once they left Gare de Modane, they were in Italy within ten minutes, and kept rolling deeper into the country. A short ride of merely an hour and a half brought them to a major train hub. Everyone on the train was convinced that they were safe at last. But for whatever reason, the refugees were kept on the train all day, with doors closed shut. No one was allowed to disembark.

As the hours passed, the people locked in the train cars grew more and more agitated. *Why are we still here?* They kept asking each other. *Why are we being kept on the train? What's happening?* Gradually the damning truth dawned on them.

Looking out the windows, to their horror, they saw German uniforms again. The Germans came there first. The Jews locked in the cars stuck on the side rail tracks outside the station, couldn't help but think of those other trains, the ones they thought they had escaped. But maybe they didn't escape. Maybe fate caught up with them. Maybe it was a ruse, and after all these years of deprivation, of hiding, of living as hunted down animals, they were lured into a trap. Maybe this time they lost this cat and mouse game. The desperation grew by the minute.

Only when night fell were they allowed off the trains. The Germans, they discovered, weren't wasting time. They had spent the day rounding up all the local Jews they could lay their hands on, going from house to house, using lists they confiscated from the local synagogue registry. They'd narrowly escaped a similar fate. If they'd been allowed off the train, they would have been rounded up along with the others.

They finally emerged from the train and found themselves at Porta Susa, the train station of Turin, historically a seat of the Kingdom of Sardinia, an architectural gem in northern Italy and home to world renowned car makers such as Fiat, Maserati and Alfa Romeo. Three times the size of Antwerp, Turin boasted a population of seven hundred thousand residents. After three years spent in outback villages comprised of a handful of houses strewn across the mountainous terrain, they were somewhat overwhelmed by the immensity of a major city.

It was dark, and they didn't know where to go. Berel was sick with fever and Malka carried him off the train. They walked the dark streets for hours, further and further south to the outskirts of the city, until they found themselves entwined in the narrow cobbled streets of Moncalieri, a pastoral neighborhood south of Turin.

They spotted a barn with a gate cracked open. It seemed to be vacant so they snuck in and dug themselves into a fragrant heap of hay. Exhausted and bewildered, they slept there throughout the night. They awoke at five in the morning from the neighing of a horse.

They brushed the hay off their clothes and continued to search for accommodations, but couldn't find any. Turin was flooded with German troops arriving from France with every additional train. Chaim Yair tried tracking down the bus that Esther took with the three little ones, but there was no clue to follow and no one to ask.

After the *aktion* the Germans carried out the day before, the Jews of Turin vanished. The Weinstein's made their way to Via Sant' Anselmo, where the Grand Synagogue of Turin, a majestic neo-Moorish palatial building inaugurated in 1884, was located. They found it desolate, in ruins, its interior intricate decorations consumed by fire from the Allied aerial bombardment a year before, in 1942.

Having nowhere to go, with German troops on every corner and not fully trusting the reliability of their forged French documents, Chaim Yair decided that they had to continue deeper into the country. They made up their minds to avoid the train station. Instead, they went to the bus station where they hailed a bus going further east, to Milan, the second largest metropolitan city, after the capital, Rome.

The Sinagoga Centrale, the magnificent Grand Synagogue of Milan on Via Della Guastalla, inaugurated only fifty years prior, in 1892, was also in ruins, destroyed during the air raid a year before. It was deserted. It was like a grand cathedral, more like a castle, with high neo-gothic windows and towering domed ceilings, filled with dust floating in pale rays of sun, and debris covering the floor. The Torah Ark, the *Aron Kodesh*, was crushed. The Torah Scrolls were gone, hopefully rescued at the last minute during the bombardment. The sinister silence was disrupted only by the flapping wings of an occasional pigeon that mistakenly flew through the broken glass and then tried to find its way out.

Exhausted, the Weinstein's sat down in the pews to rest. They had nowhere to go.

A local Jewish woman wandered in. Her home was also demolished and she also had no roof over her head. She squatted in one of the small chambers inside the synagogue. She stared at them and shook her head tearfully, in response to seeing their despondent state.

They tried to communicate but they didn't have a common language. They could barely understand each other as she spoke in a local Italian dialect and she didn't know the Yiddish that the Weinstein's spoke. They tried French and Flemish. She knew only Italian.

But they didn't need many words to understand each other. She shared with them the little food that someone had left behind, and went to look for some more in the abandoned dumpsters at the back of the synagogue. They appreciated her futile efforts to help them get something to eat.

All she managed to find was a box of *matzah* left behind from last year's Pesach, covered with mold and crawling with worms.

She gave them an address where they could find another Jew, and they set off to find him. When they met him, he brought them to someone else, walking them down the virtually deserted, debris strewn streets of Milan, passing by the ruins of buildings destroyed during the aerial raids.

"Tatteh, where are we going?" they asked their father.

"The Aibeshter knows we need a place where we can put our heads down. He will help us."

When they finally found temporary accommodations and food, they were able to rest and recover until they were ready to move on.

Everyone they met, they asked about the bus with French Jews that was supposed to arrive at Turin. Esther and the children were on that bus and it had vanished with no trace of its whereabouts. Where were they?

Days blurred into nights, into weeks and their hopes for some news were fading by the day. It seemed that the bus never arrived in Italy. No one had heard about any buses arriving from France. All lines of communication were severed.

With millions of displaced people roaming the smoldering ruins of Europe just like Chaim Yair and his children were doing, they hoped that Esther and the children who were with her were also trying to make their way, somewhere safe, somehow.

But during the dark nights that grew longer during that fateful fall of 1943, Chaim Yair shuddered.

*It's getting cold,* he thought. *How will Esther survive the coming winter?* He was too afraid to think about that other, horrific option that was lurking out there, in the back of his mind. *We made it so far,* he kept repeating to himself, and his mind would grind to a halt, unable to finish the sentence.

A month after they escaped France and set out wandering further down south, to the heartland of Italy controlled by the Allies, Chaim Yair and his children made it to Florence, halfway between Milan and Rome.

With the Germans suffering defeat after defeat on all fronts, their desperation and fanatical determination to rid the world of the Jews grew stronger with each day. The gas chambers of Auschwitz, Treblinka, Dachau and Majdanek were at their peak of destruction, and boxcars packed with Jews were rumbling in from all corners of Europe to Poland, the greatest ash receptacle of human suffering in history.

Immediately with the invasion, as if to compensate for their losses elsewhere, the Germans, aided by their Italian fascist sympathizers, raided Italian cities with renewed ferocity, in a frantic search for Jews. Every armed truck that went down the cobbled street was potentially becoming a one-way ticket to death. If they needed to flee it was becoming increasingly too difficult to run and hide with so many children.

Chaim Yair took his chances and brought his boys, Berel, Yankel and Naftoli, to Franti Minore di Montughi, the convent of the Friars of the Capuchin Order. It was located on Via Dei Cappuccini, a small street surrounded by vineyards and olive groves in the Montughi hills overlooking Florence from the north.

The convent was an assortment of rectangular two and three story buildings plainly plastered in pastel colors, strewn around a large garden with groves of olives and a well at its center. It was designated by Elia Dalla Costa, the Archbishop of Florence, as an asylum for the Jewish fugitives escaping the Nazis. When they first arrived there, they were distributed among the monasteries and convents in the area.

The next day, a nun brought the boys to Benedictine Monastero Di Santa Marta, less than a mile down the street. It was a typical sixteenth century two-story villa lining a small street on one side and flanked by an olive grove on the other.

At the peak times of their operation, the nuns were hiding no less than a hundred Jewish children. With the Nazi invasion, many children were transferred to safer locations, and only about a dozen of them remained, having nowhere to go. The nuns were willing to put their lives on the line to hide them, hoping that the Nazis wouldn't break into the houses of worship.

The nuns treated Berel, Naftoli and Yankel kindly. Naftoli went by the name Juane, Yankel as Jacques, and Berel as Bernardo. There were other orphans there, non-Jewish ones, and for the safety of everyone, Jewish names could not be uttered. The Christian children went with the nuns to a Mass in church every day, while the Jewish boys were allowed to stay in the convent and eat breakfast. Unlike clergy in other convents, these nuns didn't attempt to coerce them into Catholicism.

Even when the children had to come to the nun to kiss the cross, which they had to do in order not to arouse any suspicion, she'd cover the cross with her palm so that they'd end up kissing her hand instead.

After three years of severe malnutrition, the boys had food to eat every day: rolls with jam and coffee with milk for breakfast. It didn't take long before they started to pick up some Italian, which gave them the ability to converse and to understand the teacher in the classroom.

After all these years, learning on a daily basis was a novelty for them. Sometimes they'd get bored and restless. Sometimes they'd fall asleep, failing to grasp the intricacies of the subject matter taught in a language they barely knew. But most of the time they were intrigued to learn new things. Only now did they realize how much their brains were starved for "food for thought" – as famished as their bodies had been.

At night, when the children would lie in their beds in the large, mostly vacant dormitory hall they shared, one of the nuns would sit on a low wooden bench in the center and tell them stories from the

Bible. They'd listen to her voice echoing under the high wooden ceiling with thick beams running across it, enchanted by an exotic narrative unraveling in their imagination.

Later in life, Naftoli would tell his children and grandchildren, half in jest and half in earnest, that those childless Catholic nuns in a small convent hidden in the olive groves in the northern hills of Florence, told him magical Baal Shem Tov stories every single night.

CHAPTER THIRTEEN

## When the Eternal City Crumbles

OCTOBER 1943

Sarah and Dovid went on a scouting mission, leaving her father and her siblings behind in Florence. The newlyweds turned into a pair of vagrants, trudging on the side of dirt roads, staying overnight in deserted barns and ruins, and bargaining for scraps of food from local peasants, to sustain themselves with the few pennies they had left.

Nights were turning chilly, but the days were still pleasantly warm, and the scenery of an autumn day in Tuscany was enchanting. The disparity between the exquisitely beautiful countryside, with ripe vineyards and orchards and running hills, and despaired, famished, downtrodden humans dragging their feet on its roads, was striking. *It was an oddly dystopian honeymoon of sorts*, Sarah thought, as the beauty of tranquil sunsets in the evening would touch her heart.

Sarah and Dovid ended up staying in Rome, the seat of the Italian government and the city where the biggest Jewish community of Italy lived since the times of the Second Temple. In such a big city of one and a half million people, they had a better chance of evading detection by the Nazis or their Italian fascist collaborationists.

They sent a message to her father that he should follow them there. At that time, the Germans were tightening their grip on the north of Italy, with the help of local fascists. When the Nazis discovered that the Catholic Church was actively sheltering Jews, they began raiding monasteries and convents. Those arrested were put on trains and sent to Auschwitz, to never return.

The monastery where Berel, Yankel and Naftoli were hiding was no longer safe, and their days there were numbered. The Weinstein's had to be on the run again.

※

Chaim Yair, Malka, Miriam and Leah took a train to Rome. On their way there, the train suddenly ground to a halt, screeching with emergency brakes, cars violently shaking from one side to the other. The doors opened and people started jumping off to the gravel on the side of the tracks. All of a sudden they saw a conductor run alongside the tracks, waving to the passengers and shouting *"Scendi! Scendi! Get off!"*

A bomb planted by the *Resistanza*, the Italian partisan movement that fought the Germans and the fascists, had just exploded on the tracks, and the train was derailed.

Malka saw a well-dressed woman waving at her. She crossed over the rails and approached Malka, whose entire appearance revealed her status as a refugee, wearing patched and smudged clothing, their scant luggage tied up in a stained, worn out tablecloth instead of a suitcase, their pinched and haggard faces imprinted with that inimitable expression of hungry, hunted prey.

This was a regular train with no military personnel or cargo on it, and the fact that this woman was standing there, as if specifically waiting for the train to get stuck on that particular stretch, indicated that it was derailed for this particular reason: to give the refugees a chance to escape before they fell into the hands of the Germans swarming the train stations.

"What nationality are you?" she asked.

"We are from Antwerp," Sarah answered truthfully.

"Are you Belgian?" the woman prodded.

"Well, no. Originally my parents were from Czechoslovakia."

Her face lit up. "Perfect," she said. "There is a man in Rome who can help you. He has money for Czechoslovakian refugees. Memorize this phone number and when you come to Rome make a call from a public phone. Without idle talk just name some small street or a park in the center, whatever you choose, and the time you will be there. If someone comes to you holding a half lire, it's safe to talk to him. If not, simply run. It would mean that the phone number was compromised, the safe place was raided, and it is a trap."

The woman, a liaison from the *Resistanza*, they would later figure out, disappeared as mysteriously and as suddenly as she had emerged.

Malka memorized the number, repeating it in her head again and again, imprinting in her mind the number that could mean the difference between a chance to survive or capture and danger of death by starvation and torture.

The passengers from the train shuffled about, unsure where to go and what they should do. The train tracks weren't going to be fixed so quickly. Where should they go? Where was safe?

Ironically, their salvation would come from the Germans, the Wehrmacht troops who were not Nazi demons. In the endless torrent of human lives the most impossible encounters can happen, especially when the identities are obscured and all that's left is one human being meeting another.

Simple German truck drivers didn't have a problem giving a ride to stranded civilians, especially if there were pretty young girls among them. Any semblance of normal human presence, of people in civilian clothes, gave them the hope that the day would come when they would return to their normal lives, in the homesteads and villages of Germany.

Several open-backed military trucks pulled up, and German drivers shouted in their broken Italian with a heavy German accent *"Sali in macchina* – get into the car!"

Getting on a German military truck by his own choice was not what Chaim Yair had in mind, but he had no other option. Refusing their offer would only raise suspicion. He had to play the game, and it seemed that everyone else, regular Italian peasants, did it with no problem. It looked like it was a pretty common practice. Maybe the Germans themselves had gotten sick of their own war…

In order not to draw attention, the Weinstein's huddled in the middle with everyone. Chaim Yair was dressed in a suit and a hat. He had no choice but to shave his beard once they crossed into Italy and his face covered only with a few day old stubble, didn't mark him as a Jew. As they climbed aboard the truck, the German driver didn't seem to notice them. They didn't know what he was thinking, but perhaps he was exhausted, cursing in his heart these annoying Italians, these clumsy civilians who took so long to decide to take up his generous offer and get on his truck. Did they have another choice of what to do in the middle of nowhere?

At last everyone was seated on the floor, and he kicked in the first gear and set out on the bumpy road to Rome.

As they encountered the check post, it turned out that it was their sheer luck to sneak into the city with a military truck and not take the train with its searches and strict document checks. The Wehrmacht soldiers standing guard leafed through the driver's shipment documentation and logbook, walked around the truck and threw only a perfunctory look at the back.

"What do you have there?" they asked.

"Just some stranded civilians. The train they were on went off the rails. It's Italy, my friend," he muttered dismissively. The soldiers at the checkpoint laughed. "Yeah, everything gets stuck here," and they were waved into the city.

As they were let off at the enormous plaza facing *Roma Termini*, the main train station of Rome, they straggled to one of the narrow side streets, away from prying eyes. Malka told her father about the unusual encounter on the tracks behind the derailed train.

"Thank you for telling me. I want you to hide in the doorway of a nearby building, and if you see that I'm being jumped on, you should cross the courtyard and flee to a parallel street, and not even attempt to go after me."

Of course they agreed to do whatever their father said. Then he called their unknown contact and told him the name of a small street around the corner. It was discreet, but also allowed him to take off on a run if he felt that something was wrong. About half an hour later a car pulled up, the window rolled down and a man seated at the back, stretched out his hand with half a lira clutched in his fingers. Chaim Yair reluctantly climbed inside the car. True, the story all matched up, but he could still be walking into a trap. Was he going to be lucky twice on the same day, getting into a car and safely emerging from it?

Malka could hardly breathe the whole time her father was gone. Different possible frightening scenarios were running in her head, none of them with happy endings.

*If anything happens to our Tatteh, it's all my fault*, she thought. All these years were one long walk on a tightrope above the abyss, and one wrong move could be fatal. Trying to survive was a risky game, with high stakes, that they didn't choose to play. Minutes and hours passed by, and it felt like this long day that started in Florence would never end. She started thinking about what she was going to do next, and then, out of nowhere, her father emerged from the dusk.

He came back with a stipend that would cover their living expenses, including room and board, forty lira a person. Chaim Yair didn't know it, but the man he met was Mr. Sorani, the head of the Roman branch of DESALEM, *Delegazione Assistenze Emigranti Ebrei,* – the Jewish Emigrant Assistance Association.

Mr. Sorani, by his own account, took care of over twenty-five hundred Jewish refugees sheltered in different locations in Rome. More than once, Sorani had close, almost fatal encounters with the Nazis. Once he was even detained and tortured for ten days at the Gestapo headquarters on Via Tasso.

Sorani referred Chaim Yair to his secret liaison, consul general of Hungary in Rome, Victor Szász. Upon Mr. Sorani's referral, Viktor Szász issued documents on the spot for the Weinstein family, certifying that they were Hungarian refugees entitled to the protection of his state. Hungary was allied with Germany, which gave its citizens a status of legal alien residents.

Mr. Sorani and his people found eight small boarding houses scattered around *Roma Termini,* the ones that were willing to not look at the documents of their guests too closely and "forget" to report their arrival to the police, as required by law. As Stephan Schwamm, originally a Jewish lawyer from Vienna and DELASEM coordinator wrote later, this "complimentary service" raised the prices for the rooms above their regular going rate.

Those from Hungary, many of them Jewish, had two options in two hotels, one around the corner from the other, Hotel Albergo Salus on Piazza dell'Indipendenza 13, and Hotel Milani on Via dei Mille. Forty Jewish refugees stayed in Hotel Albergo Salus. Hotel Milani was a modest three-star hotel (and still exists today). For lack of accommodation, many families squatted in one room together.

The Sussholzes, Sarah and Dovid, got a room in the Milani hotel when they first arrived in Rome, and the Weinstein's, Chaim Yair and the three unmarried girls, were lucky to find a separate lodging at the Salus Hotel, right around the corner. At Salus, Chaim Yair met a few more Jews from St. Gervais, a village down the road from Colombiere where he had been hiding and Meir's *bris* took place.

The situation in Rome was tense. Only a couple of weeks earlier, on September 18, three hundred and fifty Jews that crossed the border to northern Italy from Saint-Martin-Vèsubie, were seized by SS troops and deported to Auschwitz. Two days before, a group of thirty-five Jews from Merano was deported to Innsbruck-Reichenau in Austria and from there to Auschwitz. News reached Rome of systematically carried out searches and mass executions of Jews in Novara and in towns around Lago Maggiore.

Then, on September 26, SS Lieutenant Colonel Herbert Kappler, chief of the German security police in Rome, seized two heads of the Jewish communities of Rome, Messrs. Dante Almasi and Ugo Foà, and gave them an ultimatum: deliver to him fifty kg. (110 lbs.) of gold within thirty-six hours, and then "nothing bad will happen to the Jews of Rome."

Cynically, the SS officer didn't even attempt to render this racketeering scheme any semblance of legality. It mirrored medieval times, when capricious rulers drowning in debt would demand ransom from the Jews, threatening them with massacres and expulsions.

The funds were quickly raised, the Nazi monster was fed with a ransom, and mysteriously, in the first couple of weeks of October, the reprisals against the Jews in Rome abated a little. German soldiers were treating civilians with decency, frequenting Jewish shops and courteously buying souvenirs and watches in the ghetto, paying full price without bargaining.

As confusing as this all was, with not knowing why the local SS command had decided to leave them alone, this twilight of reprieve gave the refugees huddling in the shadow of Nazi occupation, a glimpse of hope. They hoped that the beast would be satiated for a while, keeping itself busy with other tasks, and leave the Jews alone. They were buying time, hoping that the clock would run out on the Germans. Deception was the name of the game, and the Jews had no way to know that they were deliberately misled. They were losing in this game of smoke and mirrors.

Lifting the pressure and temporarily halting the persecutions, was a premeditated decision on the Germans' part. They decided to calm down the tension among the Jewish migrants sheltered in the slums of Rome, of which the Nazis were very much aware, and thus make sure they wouldn't be as prepared to run and hide when the order for a wholesale roundup would be issued.

One day before the ransom demand was made, the directive by German High Command to Herbert Klapper in Rome, sent from Berlin on September 25, stated, "All Jews, regardless of their nationality, age, sex, and personal conditions must be transferred to Germany and liquidated there. The success of this undertaking will have to be ensured by a surprise action and for this reason it is strictly necessary to suspend the application of any anti-Jewish measures of any individual nature, like to stir up suspicion of an imminent action among the population."

Rome felt an illusory safety, whereas insistent rumors were coming from the northern parts of Italy about the persecution against the Jews. In Florence, Nazis and their fascist collaborators didn't only search Jewish homes and businesses, but even did the unthinkable. They started raiding Catholic monasteries and convents in search of the Jewish fugitives in hiding, and even went as far as arresting Catholic nuns, a gross violation of time honored tradition to leave the clergy untouched. The Weinstein boys, Berel, Yankel and Naftoli, hiding at the Monastero di Santa Marta in Florence, were no longer safe.

Chaim Yair had to weigh the pros and cons of this rapidly shifting situation. He decided that the transient calm of Rome, as deceptive as it was, in comparison with the open hunting season that was declared in Florence, gave them a greater chance of survival. Only a week or two after their arrival in Rome, Miriam and Malka went back to Florence to get their brothers from the convent.

While in Florence, the girls met another large family of refugees.

"We're going to Rome," Malka told them. "Maybe you also should come."

Going under the radar and getting lost in such a big city as Rome, was an easier task than trying to find refuge in Florence where virtually everyone knew everyone. The family took her advice.

Years later, the mother of this family would tell Malka that her advice may have contributed to saving her family's life. In the following months it would turn out that Rome, situated closer to the Allied positions, was liberated months before Florence.

When they arrived in Rome, Berel moved in with his father and the older girls so they could give him the special care he needed to cope with his arthritis. Yankel and Naftoli stayed with kind Italian foster families.

Chaim Yair and the three older girls still spent countless hours searching for Esther and the three little ones. In those tumultuous days with no communication and millions on the run, squeezing their way through thousands of soldiers of all kinds and endless columns of military machinery, people would disappear and reappear again, get stuck with no transportation, hitchhiking with the Germans or the Allied forces, shot at and alternatively fed by this regiment or the other. The great chaos that Europe was plunged into meant enormous risks at any given moment, but also, that the most improbable circumstances might arise, and one should never give up hope.

They enjoyed a few days of transient peace. They'd walk to Roma Termini, the massive train station facing an enormous square with thousands of people from all over Italy converging on it daily, cruise the crowds and scan faces, listen to voices and names, hoping, praying to find a trace, a tiny hint, that would lead them to their mother and siblings.

In all the cities they'd passed on their travels, in all the convents they stopped overnight, they were looking, asking, inquiring, in hopes that their mother and siblings may have passed there or left a note. Any person they met, fleeing the war towards Rome, they asked and asked again, about the bus that never arrived at its destination. They asked everyone who might know something, if they ever heard of someone from Antwerp, or Colombière, or from Nantes-en-Ratier, that were on that bus, or any other identifying detail that would give the faintest glimmer of hope.

But Esther and the children had vanished. No one knew what had become of that bus full of mothers and babies.

᎒

There wasn't much to do day to day in Rome. By necessity, they picked up some Italian, haggling for food and basic items on the black market. When Pesach approached, Chaim Yair managed somehow to get a scant amount of wheat, grind it with a marble pestle in a small mortar, and bake matzos on a sheet of steel placed in an oven.

That was a memorable Pesach, never to be forgotten. Naftoli remembers the image of his father preparing the dough and the scent of baking matzos in the midst of the war. His father's face lit by the flames bursting from the oven, reminded him of their forefathers who, more than three thousand years ago, were also baking matzos, slaves in the Egyptian empire preparing for their journey into the desert. They were yearning for liberation, for the Exodus, hoping to reach the Promised Land.

Ever since, the Jews always remember the great Exodus, even in the darkest of times. The matzos – the bread of poverty, faith, and of freedom – reminded them of their great journey of survival throughout the ages, in spite of it all.

The Red Cross distributed packages that had a packet of cocoa in it.

This was a real luxury. Malka boiled water on the small electric burner that they used for cooking and accidentally bumped into the pot. The whole thing spilled on her hand, scalding her terribly.

She screamed in pain and ran to an infirmary that was a few doors past the hotel. Despite Malka's poor Italian, her need for immediate first aid for the burn was obvious. The nurse didn't ask any questions, or request an ID. She put cream on the wound, bandaged it, and told Malka to come back in a few days for a follow up exam.

They were very grateful for this expression of kindness that her family experienced from the native Italians. It was not the only time.

But then, just a few days after the boys' arrived from Florence, the bubble burst.

The first roundup in Rome was carried out by the Nazis on October 16. The operation of liquidating the Jews from Rome had begun.

Several days later they raided the Salus Hotel. Padre Benedetto, a Catholic priest and a righteous gentile who devoted his life and soul to saving Jews, "happened" to be there just then. As he saw the German troops jumping off the military trucks and converging on the Piazza dell'Indipendenza in front of the hotel, he hastily summoned all the Jews and led them to the backyard where they scaled the wall and escaped. Germans entered and started checking documents, and couldn't find a single Jew. But then other refugees, oblivious of the danger, walked right into the trap, and were detained. Father Benedetto, alone, argued with the Germans to let them go, but to no avail.

He called for Victor Szász, the Hungarian consul general who issued the fake documents that the Germans were scrutinizing now. Upon his arrival, Szász feigned fury, counting on his diplomatic immunity, lashing out at the German officer. He threatened him that if Hungarian citizens would not be granted immunity, there would be retribution against German citizens in Hungary. His threat, empty as it was, was effective, and the seventeen Jews that were detained in that *aktion* and otherwise would have certainly found themselves on the next transport to Auschwitz, were miraculously released.

But the relief was temporary. Italian fascists aligned with Hitler provided the Germans the information that came to them through local channels, about the identities and whereabouts of those helping the Jews, and establishments where Jews were hiding. SS soldiers were often accompanied by Italian fascists who helped them communicate with the staff, going from door to door and identifying the fugitives, plundering the houses and carrying out the arrests.

It became common to wake up every morning to the news of more people picked up in the night. These raids were mostly carried out by the Italian fascists, zealously doing all they could to get rid of the *ebrei*, the Jews. The Nazis, happy to delegate this messy and tedious work to others, were only overseeing the operation from afar. Sometimes they took men, women and children, sometimes they only took males. The Weinstein's, having outraced their pursuers all these years, always one step ahead of the chase, were trapped, praying they wouldn't be caught.

On December 13, 1943, Malka, Miriam, Leah, and Berel were lucky. The Italians weren't taking women and children on that particular day.

But that was the terrible day that their father was taken away from them.

The next day, Malka wanted to bring food to her father, but she didn't know where he was being held. Seeing that the arrests were carried out by Italians, she assumed it was some kind of an administrative action, a bureaucratic blunder. She thought perhaps he was in a local jail and as soon as he would come before the magistrate judge, his Hungarian passport would be enough to let him go. She was waiting to cross the street when she saw a military truck passing by. On the back of the truck, with two SS soldiers with their distinctive MP38 submachine guns drawn, there was a young Jewish girl she recognized, a beautiful redhead.

Frightened, Malka returned to the hotel. Someone must be turning all the Jewish refugees in and she could be next. She realized she wouldn't be helping her father by trying to bring him food; she'd be throwing herself into the lion's den.

Later, the family learned that Victor Szász, the heroic Hungarian consul general, the one who personally issued Chaim Yair his fake Hungarian documents and who time and time again put his life on the line to save the Jews, went down to Gestapo headquarters and intervened again. It was not a trivial thing to do, even with his diplomatic immunity.

Around the same time, a Yugoslavia consul in Rome, Cyril Kotnik, was detained and savagely tortured by the Gestapo, later to die of his wounds. Szász knew that he was putting his life at risk, but undeterred, he insisted on the release of "Hungarian nationals," and again he succeeded to have many of them released.

But Chaim Yair was not among them.

※

On that same day, they came for Dovid Sussholz. Sarah answered the door. Sarah and Dovid also had Hungarian papers. Dovid's name was listed as Andra Vajony, and Sarah was his "sister" rather than his wife.

"We are taking your brother," they said brusquely. "He's Jewish."

"Of course he's not," Sarah said.

"Let him come down to the police station with us, and we will do a background check on him," they said.

"He's sick. You can't take him," was Sarah's defiant response.

The fascists laughed. "You're a tough cookie, we can see. Fine. We will get a doctor to come," they said. "He'll do a physical examination on your brother and tell us if he is Jewish or not."

Sarah stared fiercely at them. "Aren't you ashamed of yourself?" she started yelling. In Italy, shouting matches were the norm, and a regular Italian male would not dare face a furious woman. "Even the Germans don't dare do that, to subject a decent man to such humiliation!"

Their mob mentality betrayed them. They felt strong and brave and blood-thirsty when they were ganging up on weak victims. But as soon as they met a tough lady, they stepped back and tumbled down the stairs in search of different prey.

During all that time, a fatal battle for the Italian peninsula was raging in its utmost fury. For a year and a half, from the day of Italian surrender to the Allies on September 3, 1943 and all the way until May 2, 1945, merely a week before the total capitulation of Nazi Germany and the Axis, the Italian peninsula was a war theater. During the fighting, the Allies suffered 320,000 casualties, the Axis' toll was 330,000, and Fascist Italy lost 200,000. Eight hundred and fifty thousand people, a staggering number nearing a million, were killed or missing on both sides during this operation. Germans erected a few well-fortified defense lines south of Rome, assisted by a rugged mountainous terrain that created natural obstacles for any large scale military advancement.

Between January and May 1944, four massive offensives were launched against the Gustav Line, and only in April, after months and countless lives and a great joint effort of the Allied forces from many countries – Americans, British, French, Canadians, and Polish corps – did it become clear that the fall of the German defense lines was imminent, and Rome would be liberated. As the fighting pressed closer, Rome fell within the range of Allied bombers. Germans drew the anti-aircraft batteries to the city, and it was only a question of time until the bombing would resume. Located in the very heart of the city, less than a mile away from the main train station, a prime strategic target, Hotel Salus became imminently unsafe.

But the danger awaiting them was much closer and more elusive. Bloodied, on the brink of defeat, suffering debilitating numbers of casualties and disrupted lines of supply, Germans and their Italian fascist collaborators were frantic in their last ditch effort to hunt for the Jews. They weren't able to deport anyone as the railway transportation was all but brought to a standstill, but nightly raids became more haphazard and erratic, carried out with the frenzy of a wounded animal, with people shot on the spot. Safe havens where the refugees were hiding until now were no longer safe.

The older girls discussed the situation and arrived at the conclusion that if they found shelter as far away as possible from rampant fighting and occasional raids, they could stay comparatively safe. Malka found a young priest and asked permission for her and her siblings to sleep in the convent. He gave her use of a convent at the edge of the city that was no longer in use.

Malka retrieved her siblings from the Christian families that were sheltering them, and the six of them, Miriam, Malka, Berel, Yankel, Naftoli, and Leah hid in the deserted convent. There were no beds and the place was neglected, but it felt safe. The kindly priest brought them enough food to subsist on.

Naftoli kept asking about their father. "*Vi iz Tatteh?*" he kept asking. "Where is *Tatteh*?"

"He's coming home," his sisters assured him. "He can't come now, but he's going to come." They couldn't bear to tell him the truth; that nobody came back, that their father was gone and they would probably never see him again. And the same was heart-breaking true for their mother and siblings who had disappeared without a trace.

Naftoli was still so young, how could they tell him? But he felt the truth in his heart. He heard the words, *Tatteh is coming back*, but he cried night after night, tears soaking his bed, crying for his *Tatteh* that he'd never see again. Everyone rounded up was sent to a detention camp and from there straight to Auschwitz.

In the midst of all this fear and tension, Sarah and Dovid were expecting their first child. She needed to give birth soon, and she knew that she needed help. She went with her forged Hungarian and French papers to the French delegation in Rome where Sarah was able to meet with François de Vial.

He was a well-known military *attache* in the French Embassy to the Holy See, son of the decorated brigadier general Felix Vial. His father fought against the Germans in World War I. François de Vial had been on a diplomatic mission with the French embassy in Budapest, Hungary, between 1935 and 1939, and personally witnessed the atrocities perpetrated against the Jews there.

An heir to a long line of succession of French and Spanish aristocrats, raised on values of honor and civility, François de Vial detested the brutality with which Germans hunted down people, just as his father had detested German military aggression during World War I.

When they met, Sarah sensed his genuine compassion and she told him the real truth.

"I am not really French. I am a Jew from Belgium. My father disappeared in the intestines of the Gestapo prison. We have no idea where he is and whether he is alive.

"My husband was involved with the Resistance when he lived in France, and now he is hiding from the Germans."

Sarah's intuition about François de Vial's willingness to help others was correct. He didn't tell her, but during his mission in Rome, he saved over four thousand people, both Jews and Allied servicemen, who found themselves trapped behind the German lines.

Sarah continued to pour out the story of her family's escape and survival and her uppermost concern about the upcoming birth of her baby. She was already due to give birth and didn't know where to go. He listened with a compassionate ear.

"I would like you to meet my wife," he said and introduced a very fine woman with penetrating eyes and outstanding acumen. Madame de Vial, despite her aristocratic status and the diplomatic immunity that she and her husband had enjoyed for decades, had been listening in the adjacent room. She felt great empathy and respect toward this young Jewish woman, a pregnant refugee who had been leading a life of destitution and sheer endurance for so many years.

"I will arrange for you to give birth in the clinic where diplomats go. You will have food to eat. They will treat you well. We will do what we can to help," she said in a reassuring voice.

François de Vial was the only foreign diplomat who enjoyed the privilege of free travel without needing to issue a special permit for every time he left the embassy. He and his wife drove Sarah to the clinic, thus making sure that she wouldn't be harassed by the soldiers at the check posts.

She was greeted by a midwife who welcomed her warmly and brought her into the birthing section of the clinic. Her husband wasn't with her and her father and mother weren't with her. She was very grateful to know that the diplomat and his wife stayed in the clinic while she gave birth to her baby.

When they heard that she gave birth to her son, they congratulated her. They did not have their own children, and at that moment they felt a true affinity and connection with this strong, courageous young woman and her newborn.

They graciously returned a few days later, when Sarah was going to be released from the clinic. His wife dressed the baby in infant clothes decorated with the French flag.

"We would be honored to be his godparents," she gushed.

Sarah's baby was born in the midst of Allied bombardments. The head nurse implored Sarah to baptize her baby immediately. "If he dies unbaptized, he will not attain salvation," she said.

"I need to wait for my husband," Sarah said. "I can't baptize my son without him."

The head nurse's admonitions notwithstanding, the hospital was unharmed during the air raid. Infants were a rare sight in those days filled with death and destruction. Seeing a baby cuddled in his mother's arms, instilled in people the hope that another day would surely come, that there was a future, and if their generation was broken by the atrocities it had to witness, maybe this baby would see a different, brighter world, in which people would no longer learn to kill or murder anyone.

Finding a *mohel* to perform their baby's *bris* was just as difficult, almost impossible, as it had been to find for her brother Meir's *bris*.

But when that auspicious day came, they named their baby Moshe and prayed that he would be a testament to the future that had to be better than the present.

The old convent on the outskirts of Rome where the Weinstein's found refuge, gradually filled up, as more and more people fleeing the cramped, heavily bombarded neighborhoods of the city center, sought refuge.

The fighting intensified. The Americans pressed on. The Weinstein's, huddling in the basement of the convent, heard the constant shooting and the booms of artillery for days on end. They didn't know what was going on, what to expect, whether they were going to come under carpet bombardment, as the Allies did in many cities across German occupied Europe.

Unbeknownst to them, events took a whole different turn. Instead of acting on pure military rationale and moving in to encircle and destroy the 10th German Army, General Mark Clark marched into Rome and thus engraved his name in military history as the man who liberated the Eternal City. Seizing the opportunity, the Germans abandoned Rome and announced it an "open city," which meant that they were not contesting control or attempting to defend their positions in the city. The invading army did not need to launch any military offensive like bombing or artillery shelling. They could simply march into the city unopposed and take over control.

German forces, having closely avoided decimation and surrender, escaped up north. Not being forced to lay arms, the Germans would carry on fighting, inflicting many more thousands of casualties on the Allied forces.

For this, many historians judge General Clark harshly, as a man who, by disobeying orders, caused countless more deaths to the troops under his command. Whatever the judgment of history is, his decision to race into the city instead of engaging the 10th Army, may have saved the Weinstein's' lives. Given the opportunity to escape, Germans, instead of unleashing their agonizing fury on the city they had been torturing for so long, simply ran, leaving behind the Jews they didn't succeed killing.

Finally... there was silence.

America liberated Rome from the Germans on June 14, 1944. The Weinstein children watched, from a low window in the basement, as the Germans fled the city, many on bicycles. Soon after, the Americans marched in on foot and in trucks and tanks. Malka marveled at how young and well groomed the Americans looked, so different from the haggard appearance of the people who spent five long years in a constant battle for survival.

The Weinstein's abandoned their shelter and crawled out to the street, for the first time feeling that they didn't have to fear a shout, "Halt!" or a bullet in their backs.

It was an eerie feeling, of being pardoned and released from death row. All of a sudden, there was life out there, and they were part of that life. Light was brighter, the skies seemed higher, the air was not stagnant with death, and every breath was not the last one.

The soldiers that were riding the trucks and marching down the road shared some bread and milk and canned food with the refugees. Many thousands of these soldiers would eventually die in the ensuing bitter battles of attrition where Nazis were ferociously fighting for every inch of their lost nightmarish glory, their fantasy of world dominion, their bloodthirsty vision of the New Order that took so many lives and would still take so many more. But now, on that beautiful summer day, everyone was happy. It was a bittersweet moment, a breath of fresh air that could be taken with a deep inhalation.

The Weinstein's were free. For them, the war was over.

But they had paid a huge price. Their father was gone, surely never to be seen again. And their mother and younger siblings were also still missing.

Would they ever be together again?

CHAPTER FOURTEEN

# Haven: Sailing Out of the Storm

Two weeks passed. The priest, who had kindly let the Weinstein's stay in the abandoned convent, asked them to leave. V-Day on May 8, 1945 wouldn't happen for another long year, but the battle of Rome was over. And so they found themselves on the street.

They were lucky to be alive, and now their lives were no longer in immediate mortal danger. In Italy, unlike postwar Poland and Hungary, no one deliberately targeted them for being Jews. But food shortages, lack of governance, and millions of dispossessed and despairing vagrants roaming the ruins of Europe, resulted in a chaotic and precarious situation with dangers lurking behind every corner and in every shadow.

During those summer months of 1944, across the ocean in faraway America, a series of events took place, seemingly unrelated, but they'd have a direct impact on the lives of the Weinstein children, providing them, among a group of almost one thousand refugees from Italy, with a safe haven and opening a door to a better life. The plan was called, unsurprisingly and unimaginatively, *Haven*.

Enter Ruth Gruber, a young, vivacious Jewish woman, only thirty-three years old, who had already distinguished herself by undertaking dangerous, life threatening and nearly impossible missions as a photojournalist. What she called "the most important assignment of her life" was not as a journalist on daring report assignments, but rather as a diplomat.

During World War II, she was a special assistant to the US Secretary of the Interior, Harold L. Ickes.

Ruth was so shocked when she heard about the limitation on refugees allowed to enter the United States that she dropped her coffee to go have a talk with Secretary Ickes. In her world, there were no half measures. Everything she did in life was all the way.

She was made of a different human fabric, not one for tiptoeing around challenges. She'd stare them right in the face. Secretary Ickes knew it when she stood in his office, a feisty young Jewish woman of superior wit and steely resolve. She was an inimitable mix of a Jewish American princess and a Western frontier pioneer.

"Mr. Secretary, this is what we've been fighting for all these years! To open doors. To save lives, to circumvent the holy quotas. *A meager thousand refugees?!* Out of millions whose homes were burnt down on them, whose loved ones were tortured and murdered, who were hunted down all across Europe, we can only receive a thousand people? That's all America can do?"

She knew this *Haven* plan was more of a political act than an altruistic effort to save lives. Refugees were streaming into Italy at the rate of eighteen hundred a week, getting in the way of the Allies who were struggling to force the war-crazed Germans into conceding defeat. What should have been a swift operation to finish that insane war became a yearlong series of bloody, atrocious battles of attrition.

Tens of thousands of troops would die and hundreds of thousands more would be wounded fighting battles until almost the very day the war ended. Roads flooded with refugees made military maneuvering very difficult, and the task of rooting out the Germans even harder. Someone had to deal with the "refugee problem" and get rid of the road clogging, tank obstructing logistical and humanitarian nightmare.

Even after the president acquiesced to US military pressure, agreeing to resettle the evacuees, he was still reluctant to roll out the red carpet. Instead, he pushed to create offshore havens in Europe, Sicily, or North Africa.

Later, Gruber discovered the primary prompter of the decision, a shady secret that the United States of America, a shining castle on a hill of democracy, tends to forget. The American establishment at that time was thoroughly anti-Semitic and some even sympathized with the Nazis. The plight of the Jewish Holocaust didn't stir their hearts, and they weren't willing to let the European Jews in. Buried under the rubble of war and deflected by the heroic, sacrificial effort of the American military in its fight against the Nazi machine – so the establishment believed – their hostile apathy to the genocide of European Jewry would not be remembered or held against them.

But the paper trail always retains the uncomfortable reality that is hard to deny.

A series of horrifying 1942 cables – suppressed by the State Department for over two years – had somehow made its way to the Treasury Department, then led by Henry Morgenthau, a Jew who was fully assimilated into American society but had a warm and vibrant Jewish heart. The cables described Hitler's atrocities in agonizing detail, including the systematic use of Zyklon-B in eliminating European Jewry. American intelligence knew, American top brass knew, American top echelons of power knew.

And they did nothing.

During the war, American Jews rationalized the limited quotas of refugees by making themselves believe that the Jews back in the Old World, across the ocean – denied asylum on American shores – suffered just like any other civilian population in a war-ravaged region, on par with the French or Italian farmers and city dwellers, facing the regular difficulties of food rations and curfews, sustaining the collateral damage of vast military operations, and maybe taking body blows of millennia old anti-Semitism. No one imagined that their brothers and sisters were systematically exterminated in a massive genocide beyond comprehension in its horror. No one even yet knew the extent of the torture in an industry of mass slaughter well-funded and meticulously run with devote dedication to a transportation network and "disposal" system.

Jews in America, comparatively successful, but still conscious of widespread anti-Semitism, danced at charity balls and collected money for their relatives who were tragically trapped in the war that raged in Europe. But they were not yet aware of the reality on the ground, the concentration camps, mass executions, death marches, the round ups and cattle cars transporting millions into the ovens of Auschwitz, Treblinka, Bergen Belsen, and dozens of other extermination camps.

No one knew, and American intelligence and political class intentionally suppressed this information from the general public. Moreover, as it turned out, the US State Department, with full knowledge of the extent of human catastrophe, was intentionally acting to deny the financial and operational support that was authorized for the Jews of Europe.

A group of young Jewish lawyers at the Treasury Department, among them John Pehle, director of the Treasury Department's foreign funds control, and Josiah E. DuBois, who later would go on to become one of the prosecutors at the Nuremberg Trials, found evidence that the State Department had actively suppressed information about the genocide of the European Jews and obstructed efforts to help them. They wrote a position paper, first drafted by DuBois, entitled, unequivocally and harshly, "Report to the Secretary on the Acquiescence of this Government to the Murder of the Jews." This report avoided attributing motives, whether it was good old anti-Semitism or uniquely American isolationism, both mainstay features of the American public opinion and foreign policy during WWII. The report didn't shy away from stating the facts and putting the blame squarely at the door of the State Department.

The bottom line of that report delivered fully on its damning title. While the Treasury Department had granted the World Jewish Congress permission to send the money to Switzerland in July 1943, the State Department used various excuses to delay the implementation of this relief program until December that year, a full eight months after the program was first proposed. This report, gruesome in its graphic, blood curling detail, was presented to Henry Morgenthau Jr., the Secretary of Treasury and a personal friend of President Roosevelt.

"Morgenthau read DuBois's eighteen page report with mounting rage," Ruth Gruber wrote in her book *Haven*, documenting those life-changing days.

"I am physically ill," Henry Morgenthau said, in agony, after reading the memorandum. Even he, at the top echelons of American politics, was shocked by the revelations of Nazi atrocities. But no less was he sickened by the suppression of information and by the openly anti-Semitic, sinister policy of the State Department.

On January 16th, 1944, Henry Morgenthau, accompanied by John Pehle and a few other lawyers from his department, marched into the Oval Office. He was filled with fury and pain. Still, reason took over, and he renamed the report to an understated "Personal Report to the President." Not the title, but the content of the report, had to shake the President up.

This Oval Office meeting was a culmination of a highly publicized and persistent campaign to help the Jews of Europe, spearheaded by the Bergson Group and assisted by such prominent figures as the President's wife, Eleanor Roosevelt, leading senators and congressmen, and Hollywood and Broadway celebrities.

Shockingly, the political figures that supported this plan were representing only the states and districts with no significant Jewish population. This ostensibly marginal fact that is easy to overlook, underscores the inconvenient truth of those days: Anti-Semitism was so widespread and deeply entrenched in the minds of the public that the politicians holding office in regions where Jews were a known entity were reticent to show too much support for their cause, in fear of alienating their non-Jewish constituencies. This general anti-Jewish and isolationist sentiment also explains why President Roosevelt needed so much pressure to take action.

"On this Sunday morning, he was no longer Henny-Penny," wrote Ruth Gruber in *Haven*, referring to the president's nickname for his money man Henry Morgenthau. "He had become a committed, anguished, passionate Jew. The suppressed cables had touched ancient roots."

That encounter behind closed doors at the White House, no doubt a charged one, with raw emotions shown and harsh words said, tipped the scale and resulted in the issuing of a Presidential Executive Order number 9417, entitled "On Creating the War Refugee Board."

The Presidential Executive Order, circumventing the US Congress, was needed because the Congress refused to pass the law lifting the quota on the Jewish refugees admitted into the country.

This order was issued on January 22, 1944, and made public by the media the day after. Roosevelt emphasized, in a not so veiled rebuke at the US Congress, and at his own obstructionist State Department bureaucrats, that it was urgent that action be taken at once to forestall the plan of the Nazis to exterminate all the Jews and other persecuted minorities in Europe.

During the next few years the War Refugee Board would be credited with rescuing tens of thousands of Jews from Nazi-occupied countries, operating by proxy of the Swedish diplomat Raoul Wallenberg and others.

Appallingly, this was the one and only major effort undertaken by the United States government to save the lives of Jews during the Holocaust. Even more atrociously, other governments did even less. Silent acquiescence with the genocidal Nazi practices toward the Jews was prevalent policy of all governments, including the British who, in spite of their aerial bombardments of German occupied territories, did nothing to destroy the railways that led hundreds of thousands of innocent Jews to the concentration camps of Auschwitz and Treblinka. One or two air raids could've brought to a halt the entire industry of extermination and possibly saved the lives of millions. Paradoxically, one of the improbable, inconceivable truths of WWII is that the Italians – members of the Nazi Axis, no less – did more to save Jews during that war than the Allies did.

Ruth Gruber was an unstoppable, daring, no holds barred photojournalist who traveled to the most challenging and dangerous corners of the world to bring back chilling pictures and firsthand accounts of what was happening in the world out there. She entered the scene with a mission to educate and make changes. She was a spunky daredevil, not afraid to take risks to make a powerful point. In her mid-twenties, a few years before the war broke out, she had traveled to the Soviet

Arctic as a foreign correspondent, entering millions of square miles of extreme weather, icebergs, permafrost and the Gulags of Stalinist Russia. Two years after the war, she would cover the arrival of SS Exodus 1947, a ship carrying more than forty-five hundred Jewish refugees from the Holocaust fighting their way through the British blockade into Palestine. Later in life, when she was a woman in her seventies, she would go on to report on the Mossad operation of rescuing the Jews in Ethiopia and their clandestine voyage to Israel.

"The words leaped at me from The Washington Post," she would recount many years later, reading the announcement of President Roosevelt in which he stated, 'I have decided that approximately one thousand refugees should be immediately brought from Italy to this country.'

"One thousand refugees.... for years refugees knocking on the doors of American consulates abroad have been told, 'You cannot enter America. The quotas are filled.' And while the quotas remained untouchable... millions died."

Ruth knew instantly that this was going to be her next assignment. She was going to step right into the fire consuming Europe and salvage as much as she could from the ocean of misery and destruction.

"The people that are coming here must be frightened, bewildered, overwhelmed by coming to a strange land," she said to Harold Ickes. "Somebody has to be with them on their journey. Somebody has to take their hands."

She had a dynamic and fearless personality, a proven record as a photojournalist who ventured on missions in extreme conditions, knowledge of Yiddish and German, and impressive academic credentials, awarded a fellowship in German Literature in 1931 at the University of Cologne, Germany, at the age of twenty, becoming the world's youngest PhD at the time.

Ruth Gruber was perfect for the job.

Similar to her voyage to the Soviet Arctic, only more dangerous, she was tasked with the secret mission of traveling to Europe, in the midst of the ever changing warfare landscape of WWII, and escorting the one thousand refugees from Italy to the USA, across the fatally dangerous Atlantic Ocean. As she said later, this was her "defining Jewish moment."

Interior Secretary Harold Ickes granted her a "simulated rank of general," so that if the seaplane she was going to cross the Atlantic in was shot down and she'd fall into German captivity, she would be treated not as a civilian of Jewish descent, which would mean a bullet straight to her head right on the spot, but as a high ranking POW. In this way her life would be protected under the auspices of the Geneva Accords – if the Germans chose to respect it.

Toward the end of the war, more Wehrmacht officers were inclined to oblige with international law, knowing that soon enough they would be standing trial for crimes against humanity. Having a high profile witness, whose life they spared, take a stand for them could be their life insurance.

Ruth Gruber took that flight into the inferno.

❦

Word of the President's Executive Order spread like brushfire and people knocked on the US consulate doors day and night.

"There were men and women weeping, people fainting from emotion, parents holding their children up in the air so we'd notice them," recounted Max Perlman, one of those who screened the refugees.

"You can't imagine the emotional excitement that was electrifying the air. Some of the men made long speeches telling me how many years they had been dreaming about going to America. Others just wept openly... I couldn't tell them if they'd be accepted or not. There were many men who were all alone; they had seen their entire families wiped out... the pain in their faces is still with me."

Eight hundred and seventy-four of the nine hundred and eighty-two handpicked refugees were Jewish. Roosevelt was weary of being framed as peddling the Jewish cause and didn't want it to be called a "Jewish rescue project." At the crossroads of big politics and ordinary lives, even the small letters mattered and certain things were better not said or done. For example: saving Jews. Either way, under this

Presidential Executive Order, an overwhelming majority of those granted asylum would have been Jewish victims of Nazi genocide.

※

Malka Weinstein and her siblings were prime candidates for this program, yet they weren't knocking on any doors. How could they leave when they still didn't know where their parents were?

When the first possibility would present itself, they were sure that their father would certainly come back searching for them, and what would happen if he couldn't find them? This was not an option. They had to stay in Europe and wait for news. While everyone was clamoring to go, the Weinstein children restrained themselves and held back. They were not emotionally ready to accept that the rest of their family may have perished in the ovens of the crematoria.

One of the organizers heard that there were six abandoned children, alone, without any adult. He came to find Malka.

"Don't be foolish," he told her. "Go to America. It's much safer there. You've made it this far, you must make sure your siblings won't get caught in the crossfire or die of famine. In any case, Roosevelt announced that under this order you will stay in the United States only until the hostilities are over. As soon as the war ends, you will be sent back here, and then you will continue to search for your mother and father."

Malka tried to weigh his words as objectively and rationally as possible and couldn't come up with a reason why she should decline it. So the Weinstein children were put on the list. But Sarah, the only married one, wasn't granted a permit. When she and her husband Dovid tried to get one of the coveted spots, they were turned down. Ironically, what saved Dovid from the Germans now worked against him. Each potential refugee was interviewed to make sure that no German spies would sneak into the country. When the interviewers heard that Dovid evaded arrest when all the residents of the hotel he lived in were arrested by the Italian Fascists, they suspected him of using his German citizenship to avoid the deportation. All German citizens were denied entry. They were automatically viewed as potential spies and perpetrators of war crimes, or at the very least they were suspected of cooperating with the Nazi regime.

Awareness of his Jewish identity and the Nazi's wrath against the Jews didn't help him. Sarah, Dovid, and their son Moshe were transferred by a refugee relief and rehabilitation organization (later to be reorganized into a UN refugee agency, UNRRA) to a refugee camp in Bari in southeast Italy.

After the war ended, the Sussholzs moved thirty miles southwest of Bari, to the very tip of the heel of the Italian Peninsula, and settled in Castignano Del Capo, a small village two miles off the Mediterranean coast. Eventually, they would return to Antwerp.

In 1945, while they were in Castignana Del Capo, Sarah gave birth to a daughter. They named her Raquela.

After the birth, while Sarah was recuperating in the hospital, Dovid was home with one-year-old Moshe.

One day he heard a knock on the door.

"Who is it?" he asked, suspecting nothing.

"We need help," he heard a male voice say in Yiddish.

Dovid opened the door and three masked men broke in. They looked menacing. Dovid, clutching his baby son to his chest, was stricken with horror. The Italian *banditi* started rummaging through drawers, unceremoniously throwing clothes and kitchenware around, rifling through all their possessions, searching for valuables.

But they found nothing. Dovid and Sarah were penniless, destitute refugees subsisting on the meager stipend provided by the Joint. Dovid slowly put his young son into his crib and forced himself to keep his breathing even, hoping they'd leave when they realized there was nothing to take. It seemed that the robbers were going to walk away empty handed, having left only havoc in their wake, but sparing the lives of Dovid and his son.

But then the mask fell off one of the men and with a flash of recognition Dovid realized who they were. They were not Italian gangsters. They were fellow Jewish refugees with whom he and Sarah once shared the little they had for a meal in their own home.

The Sussholz's had never had very much, but they had opened their home to those who were even less fortunate. These men had come for one of those meals and must have assumed that they were well off in those desperate times if they could serve food to others.

The robber whose mask fell off instantly realized that Dovid must have recognized him. In a fit of the cold murderous rage of a downtrodden wreck of a human being who had lost his last vestige of morality, he drew a dagger and stabbed Dovid time and again. In those days of rampant atrocity, many showed great heroism and self-sacrifice for the lives of others, as Dovid himself did, but many lost their faith in morality, and with it their own image of G-d.

"Please!" Dovid cried, bleeding, in an excruciating agony of pain and anguish, fearing not so much for his own life, but for the lives of those who depended on him. "Don't kill me," he pleaded. "I survived the war, survived the horror of it all. The Nazis held me at gunpoint and I survived. The war is over for us," he begged, losing blood, life pouring out of him, fainting, at his last breath. "I found my mother. She is in Belgium. I told her I'm alive. She can't lose me again."

Somehow, against all odds, his words touched something deep inside, a dormant sense of humanity that was long lost in them. They spared him the fatal blow, making him swear not to turn them in to the police. If he disobeyed and the police came looking for them, they'd know how to find him. Fear of retribution was their insurance policy. They retreated, leaving him to bleed to death, with twelve stab wounds to his chest, arms, and shoulders, abandoned to his fate, barely alive, lying on the floor in a puddle of blood.

Somehow he gathered his last drop of determination, the sheer willpower of a man who had been fighting for the six longest years of his life for his physical survival, against all odds, and staggered out to the street where a passerby found him and rushed him to the hospital. There he pleaded with them to please get his one year old son, who he had left behind and please find someone to watch him as his wife was in the hospital with their newborn. Extremely weak from his severe loss of blood, he then lost consciousness while he received critical emergency first aid treatment to stop the bleeding. No blood transfusions were available in civilian hospitals. All blood was in high demand. It was allocated to the wounded soldiers on battlefields, not to an individual stabbed in a criminal attack.

When he finally regained consciousness, the doctor said, "I am sorry to tell you that the nerves and tendons in your arm were damaged beyond repair. I do not believe that you will ever be able to use your arm again."

Dovid could not be released from the hospital until his body had recovered enough from the shock. And when he was able to be discharged from the emergency room, he took extra care to hide his bandages under his shirt and jacket before he went to his wife Sarah.

He couldn't move his arm and suffered excruciating pain, but he did not want her to know about the entire incident, his numerous injuries and his close brush with death. She was the mother of their new baby and she needed to recuperate and gain her strength for them to go on into the future.

Sarah didn't need to see his wounds to know that something horrible must have happened.

"I had a terrible feeling of dread and uneasiness that night," she said to him. "I knew."

Resilient as he was during the war, Dovid spent endless hours restoring movement to his arm, defying the pain. The recovery demanded great effort and progress was painstakingly slow. First he fought through the pain to move his paralyzed fingers again, bit by bit restoring their sensation and mobility. Then he started rotating the palm, and then slowly, gradually bending and flexing his forearm, just a tiny bit, every day fighting for another inch to expand the range of his movement.

The physical scars stayed with him forever, reminding him and his children and grandchildren of the miracle of his survival. Decades later, during the cold nights or in anticipation of rain, the wounds would ache with dull, teeth gnawing pain, reminding him of the war, that endless battle of survival, one minute at a time, when millions of people clashed in an epic collision, bringing about the destruction of spirit, of soul, of life.

Sometimes he wondered, were these the old stab wounds that

ached, or his injured soul, bleeding with loss and grief for those who perished, for those whose spirit and body betrayed them, for those who were betrayed by others, who went into the darkness and never returned.

Those endless nights...

CHAPTER FIFTEEN

# Land of the Free

Five hundred and twenty-five men and four hundred and fifty-seven women were the number of the lucky few. Out of millions scattered all across war – ravaged Europe, these were the ones who were brought into the United States under the Roosevelt Executive Order. They were interviewed, selected and then transferred to Aversa, Italy, a picturesque town of merely thirty thousand, ten miles north of Naples.

In Aversa, the refugees were housed in three spacious buildings surrounded by a lush garden. This place, formerly known as Maddalena Mental Asylum, was established in the early 19th century and gained acclaim for its outstanding care and humane attitude toward the mentally ill, where both human souls and gardens were tended with love. In the beginning of the tumultuous 20th century, the fortunes of Italy and together with it of Maddalena Asylum, dwindled.

The asylum shut its doors and the compound stood abandoned for years. Now it was given a new, albeit short life, as a temporary safe haven for those who survived the atrocities of the war, who had seen the horrors that the former residents of this place could only conjure up in their wildest delusions, persecuted by demons of their own tormented souls. But the purgatory brought upon mankind by the political madness of Nazi Germany exceeded the most extravagant nightmares of those poor souls.

In July 1944, the nine hundred and eighty-two refugees took a short ride to Naples and boarded the United States Army transport ship Henry Gibbins, part of a convoy of fourteen cargo ships carrying American wounded troops and Germans POWs, and fifteen warships, twenty-nine vessels in total, on their way to the United States shores.

The Atlantic Ocean was swarming with notoriously deadly U-boats, the German submarines, whereas the skies roared with the Messerschmitts, German twin-engine heavy bombers far superior to their Allied rivals. The Nazis would indiscriminately attack all maritime vessels, civilian and military alike, which caused hundreds of thousands of fatalities.

During WWII the U-boats alone accounted for almost three thousand drowned Allied vessels, the vast majority of them – two thousand eight hundred and twenty-five – merchant and civilians ships. It was an open season on the Atlantic.

Therefore, as a precautionary measure, the USAT *Henry Gibbins* was flanked on both sides by two cargo ships filled with German POWs. If the Nazis were to attack the convoy, they'd risk drowning their own before they got to the Americans and the refugees.

The refugees shared the ship with hundreds of wounded American soldiers. This coexistence brought about a contradictory mix of encounters, many of them heartwarming, but others were chilling reminders of how common and widespread hatred and prejudice against Jews was, crossing nations and continents.

In her book *Haven*, Ruth Gruber recounts a poignant incident during the sailing that bore open the scars and made the tragedy of the Jewish people so inescapable, so close to home. The ship was chased by a German U-boat. The engines were halted, to reduce the sonar footprint so that the submarine radars couldn't pick up the exact location of the ship and target it with its deadly torpedoes. Everyone, soldiers, refugees, the crew, were lying on their bunks paralyzed with blood curling fear, waiting for the explosion that would hurl them to the seabed. And then Ruth heard one of the American soldiers cursing at her, "it's all because of you and your Jews." The bitter irony of this situation struck her, she wrote, how fear evokes the worst in people, so that in a moment of desperation one victim of an atrocity turns on the other.

But luckily, the positive far outweighed the negative. Conditions on the ship were far from luxurious, with triple-tiered canvas hammocks for sleeping, overcrowded quarters and plain, stale food. But for the refugees who had just escaped the burning gehinnom of Europe, it was more than enough. Even the ever-present danger of predatory submarines and enemy aircraft didn't unsettle them too much. They were used to being hunted. But unlike in Europe, here they had a place to sleep and food in abundance – and they were hurrying away from the danger zone.

American soldiers shared food with the refugees, mountains of it. Goulash, frankfurters, boiled potatoes, cooked onions, salmon, salad, bread, cookies, Jell-O, and more. Sadly, many of the refugees were too sick to eat. They suffered from such an acute state of chronic malnutrition that their bodies were barely able to digest food.

As a token of appreciation for the heroic service and sacrifice of the United States troops, and to alleviate the boredom and flare up of tension, Ruth arranged an onboard entertainment, kind of ad-hoc shows for the troops and the refugees alike. Leo Mirković, in his former life a celebrated lead baritone of the National Opera House in the pre-war Zagreb, and now merely a skeletal figure dressed in a clownish, oversized, colorless robe, which was once an expensive silk suit tightly hugging his belly with its striking glistening white hue, was more than happy to show his gratitude to the troops, most of them half his age, some missing limbs, all of them irretrievably missing their childhood.

On an upper deck of a ship in the heart of the Atlantic ocean Leo gave his heart and his voice to those who came across the world to rescue him, and they, those brave kids in fatigues, were squinting against the sun, happy to be alive, laughing and singing an aria from Figaro in unison. The words were surprisingly fitting for the circumstances, floating above the waves, taking them to the safe shores of America.

*Ah, bravo Figaro!*
*Bravo, very good!*
*I am the luckiest, it's the truth!*
*Ready for anything,*
*Night and day,*
*I'm always on the move.*

They were the luckiest, so far. They were "always on the move" indeed, chased by Messerschmitts and U-boats. And yes, they were "ready for anything," even the very worst, on a moments' notice.

※

Several nights into their journey, German planes were sighted. Nine-year-old Naftoli hurried to put on a life jacket, fear palpable in everyone on the ship. He lay with his siblings on a bunk, absolutely still. Then a thick black smudge burst through the holds. People began coughing, choking, some crying out in panic. They were sure the ship was hit by an explosive dropped by a German bomber, and now they would inexorably go down to the bottom of the sea. Two military police wearing gas masks raced to calm down the refugees stricken by sheer hysteria.

"It's smokescreen," one said. "The escort warships blacked us out. But the boys who were supposed to close the vents panicked and ran downstairs, so the smoke came through our vents. We are fixing it, but you have to be absolutely still."

On more than one occasion, the ship's sonar would detect a U-boat deep under the water, searching for prey. Every time this happened they were ordered to remain silent. The engines would be turned off, and the ship would lay still, motionless, rocking on the waves without a single sound, as if it was a ghost merchant ship from the eighteenth century with a crew completely decimated by an epidemic.

But no one complained. As inconvenient and scary as it was, it was a far cry from the horrific countless stories of families hiding in cellars for endless months, a dozen people squashed into a few square feet, in total darkness, with barely any food and nothing to do, unable to talk. In desperation, families were often forced to do the imaginable and strangle their own babies to death so that their cries wouldn't reveal their whereabouts to the Nazis and doom them all. Compared to that, the Henry Gibbins scurrying across the Atlantic to America was a luxury cruise ship, with plenty of food, sunshine and fresh salty air blowing into their faces.

Naftoli and the other children spent most of the day on deck enjoying the sun. The American soldiers sat on their side of the deck, usually smoking and talking among themselves in English, which Naftoli couldn't understand. Initially the soldiers kept to themselves, viewing the refugees as a foreign, alien group of people who they had nothing in common with, not even a common language. But gradually, as it usually happens with human beings being forced to spend time in each other's company, this made them warm up to each other.

Soldiers, who were far from their own younger siblings, would feed these hungry, hunted down children, many of them suffering from stunted growth caused by malnutrition and lack of sunshine. They would play with them and teach them a few sentences in English. A child's innocence and thirst for connection would open any heart, even a heart hardened by the killing fields of the bloodiest war in human history.

For Naftoli these soldiers were warm and friendly, simple boys from the American heartland. It was the first time he'd seen someone chewing gum and he watched the soldiers chew it with great interest. They offered him a natural wonder, an exotic fruit that was both sweet and sour. Delicious juice dripped down his chin from this fruit that he'd never seen before in his life: a grapefruit.

It was all part of a new life for him, a life that he hadn't even dreamed he would live to have.

---

Their sea voyage lasted seventeen days. When lower Manhattan and the Statue of Liberty came into sight, people stood on the deck and cried. They'd escaped the trains and the chimneys of Auschwitz, the firing squads and the mass graves in the forests, the bombs raining from the skies and the U-boats preying upon them on the seas. They were no longer trapped animals in a jungle of Nazi ideology. They were human beings who had the right to live. They were safe.

"We lived through our own Yetzias Mitzrayim. A true Exodus. That's what it was and always will be," Naftoli recounts.

Little did they know that during those very days as they were approaching the United States territorial waters, the war effectively over for them, on August 1st, 1944, the Warsaw Uprising would begin. This was going to be a long and bloody year, during which almost the entire Hungarian Jewry would perish, eight hundred thousand in total, and hundreds of thousands more would still be gassed and savagely murdered all across Europe.

Could it really be that the Weinstein's were safe?

When they arrived at the American port, on August 3, 1944, the USNS *Henry Gibbins* docked on the Hudson River. The American soldiers disembarked first. They descended into small boats that took them to the shallow waters of the port. Then the boats returned and took the refugees to an island connected to the riverbank by a long bridge – Ellis Island.

They weren't given American citizenship. Having no fitting legal definition, they wore tags that listed them as "US Army Casual Baggage," an odd and somewhat chilling definition for human beings. For so long they were deemed damaged human material destined for destruction, and now again they were dehumanized by being labeled as "baggage," and "casual" at that.

Were they a burden? Were their lives a casual matter? Did they matter at all? But they didn't fuss over such trivial matters. They were alive and so far no one attempted to kill them. They were exceedingly grateful to have escaped the fate they would have faced in Europe. They signed the papers, agreeing to extradition back to Europe after the war ended.

The first thing Naftoli noticed as they got off the boat on that Friday morning, were the cars. "Gee," he said, "There are so many cars here."

He hadn't seen many cars in Antwerp or France. They had left a whole different era behind them, still inhabited by horses and carriages.

Unfortunately, though it may not have been intended, the refugees were treated more like cattle than dignified human beings. They were being "processed," not cared for.

First, they were taken into a large room and ordered to remove their clothes. Then they were sprayed with a disinfectant. This was a precautionary medical procedure, done to protect against the epidemic of typhus that was sweeping across Europe and killing countless numbers. American immigration officers were just doing their job, preventing possible diseases from being brought to the United States shores. They could not have known that for some of the refugees who were imprisoned in the concentration camps, this procedure reminded them of the horrors of selection.

It wasn't just the accidental similarity that hit them, but a very tangible sense of an all-pervading terror, revisiting in full color one of the most horrifying moments in their very recent past. Some burst in tears, some were hit by a momentary bout of hysteria, unable to fight the onslaught of flashbacks that were inexorably flooding them.

But then, after the process of registration, disinfection and medical examination was completed, the refugees were given decent clothes, not striped uniforms, and normal food and donuts. They weren't given the watery murky substance called "soup" that had been a staple of concentration camps rations.

After all of this "processing," the refugees were taken straight on a twenty-four hour long trip on a train up north to Schenectady, in upstate New York, and then transferred to a westbound train to Syracuse. From there they were bussed to Oswego, a hamlet on the southeastern shore of Lake Ontario. With its barbed wire, rows and rows of wooden barracks and military patrols, the abandoned and hastily refitted Oswego army fort looked too similar to a concentration camp for comfort.

Yet they soon realized how far away they were from that terrible reality. Unlike the hostile, hatred filled residents of Oświęcim, the Polish town neighboring Auschwitz, Oswego residents passed bread and milk to them through the gates, all smiles. Some handed toys, clothing, and even a bicycle over the fence.

The Weinstein family was placed in a winterized barrack, with three bedrooms to house them all. It was simple but clean and comfortable.

They were happy to be alive, to be safe, to cherish the joys of children. Having their first ice cream was pure delight. A picture was snapped of them as a group of children smiling to the camera, holding cones of ice cream. This picture, so trivial at the first glance, encapsulated their entire story of unimaginable tragedy, of survival, of the miracle of life, and of an indestructible hope.

Because such an unusual story rested behind such a seemingly ordinary picture, this photograph was featured in the *Aufbau*, a German Jewish publication.

Some of the refugees resented the month long quarantine and the limits imposed by the authorities on their freedom to work or leave Oswego. But most just were grateful to be.

"Being confined didn't bother me at all," Naftoli reminisced. "We weren't bored and we were not confined to the perimeter of the barbed wire. We were in school during the week. On Sundays we got to go around town. We had sports, we had food, we had shelter. We even had a house with steam that kept us warm and provided us with hot water.

"A shipment of shoes and clothing from Agudath Israel was sent to Oswego. I got a winter coat. It was warm, with a hood. I also got proper leather shoes. Until then, I was wearing paper shoes."

Oswego swarmed with reporters when the refugees first arrived on August 4. Here was a chance to hear about the war firsthand from those who had been there. Here were survivors from the European inferno that was still consumed by flames, who had experienced it firsthand, who bore witness to the collapse of civilization. They could give those stories that sounded too grotesque to be true, their real, human face.

American Jewry was waking up to the reality of the nightmare called the Holocaust.

A reporter from the Yiddish "Morgen Journal" interviewed Berel (Bernard) upon his arrival, and the article was published a few days later, on August 9, 1944.

August 9th, the day the interview with Berel Weinstein was published, was the day the SS and Gestapo began liquidating the Litzmannstadt Ghetto in Lodz, transporting its inhabitants to Auschwitz-Birkenau. Ultimately, two hundred thousand Jews of Lodz Ghetto would be murdered. Also, on that very day another shipment of sixty thousand Jews was making its way to the same sinister destination, Auschwitz. Tragically, as the American readers were skimming the touching story of little Berel Weinstein during their morning coffee, cattle cars were thundering across Europe into the black smoke of crematoriums.

The Holocaust ravaged Europe for years, and it was still far from being over, but the Jews of America were only getting their first glimpse of it. It was a harrowing, gut wrenching story that had to be told.

Another newspaper interviewed Miriam, painstakingly trying to make sense of the raw, inconceivable horror of broken families and broken lives on the other side of the ocean. The reporter concluded with an impassioned appeal that was published for all to read:

Despite witnessing the depravity of evil – or maybe because of it – many of the refugees didn't lose faith. Out of the eight hundred and seventy-four Jewish refugees settled in Oswego, about a hundred of them were religious. They made a great effort to restore an active religious life, building a *shul*, a *mikvah* and a kosher kitchen.

Mr. Jacob Dresdner, a *chassid* from a small town straddling the Hungarian-Romanian border Satu Mare, today known in the Jewish world as Satmar, led the prayers in *shul* and read from the Torah.

Oswego camp was an experiment in communal life, only instead of a bare fisted fight for survival it was an effort to live as a community, as a good society. The Weinstein's were there from August 4, 1944, until January, 1946.

They ate all their meals together with the other families in the barrack designated as a dining room. When the holiday of Succos approached, Naftoli decorated the communal *sukkah* they all shared. These were the first days of October and the weather was pleasant, unusually warm for the season, climbing as high as 79 degrees.

And in the spring, in the last days of March, 1945, with the war back in Europe entering its final, victorious stage, they celebrated communal Pesach Seders together.

Naftoli and all the children chanted out loud, the words of the *Ma nishtana* that reverberated into the warm night with gusts of wind blowing from Lake Ontario. The entire camp, religious and secular alike, held their breath, assembled together, on that unforgettable night commemorating the Exodus from Egypt, the celebration of the Jewish people's first historical liberation as a nation. Everyone was deeply moved, enraptured by the raspy voices of children singing about their own Exodus, no less dramatic perhaps than the original one, as they were rescued from the most recent and the worst nightmare humanity had ever encountered.

While the Weinstein's lived at Oswego, Malka and Miriam were active in organizing beautiful *mesibas Shabbos* parties for the children that celebrated the beauty of Shabbos. The previous Lubavitcher Rebbe, Rabbi Yosef Yitzchak Schneerson, *zt"l*, wrote a general letter of *chizuk*, of emotional support, to the refugees there, and a special letter addressed to Malka and Miriam Weinstein, thanking them for their efforts making these vital *mesibas Shabbos* for the children.

After their first month of quarantine, the children were assigned to local schools. Malka was ecstatic to get back behind a desk. She hadn't been to school for so many years and she was desperate to catch up, to make up for lost time, to quench her thirst for knowledge that was stifled for all those years of strife and wandering.

She sat at a desk in high school soaking up as much as she could, absorbing English at a lightning speed. When she was forced to make do attending the sewing school of the ORT, what she dreamt about the most was finding herself again in a regular school, studying regular academic subjects, exploring her horizons, honing her intellectual acumen. She had vowed that if the war wouldn't take her life and she would emerge from it sound and well, she would go back to school, no matter her age. Now her dream was coming true.

The boys went to public school in the first part of the day. In the afternoons *Yeshivah Torah Vodaath,* originally established in 1918 in the Lower East side and then moved to Williamsburg, Brooklyn, arranged for one of its alumni, a young man named Reb Naftoli Eller, to move to Oswego and teach the boys Jewish subjects in an afternoon Talmud Torah, from *alef-bais* to Talmud.

It was a genuine Yiddishkeit, like in the old country. They heard Jewish stories and learned *Chumash* with Rashi commentary, and the weekly *parshah* Torah portion.

Naftoli was a toddler when WWII broke out. He never had a chance to go to a *cheder* and get a taste of the ancient tradition of Jewish learning. He cherished this opportunity to become part of an experience sanctified by time and countless generations of his predecessors, immersing himself in the ocean of Torah. This Talmud Torah was Naftoli's first opportunity to be exposed to the formal learning of his Torah heritage and the Torah way of life.

Reb Eller taught them inspiring classes in the Yiddish language and one major subject was learning to translate the *Chumash* from Hebrew into Yiddish.

Naftoli still recalls these lessons decades later.

Reb Eller had twenty children to teach. He arranged them into separate classes according to age and level. "We didn't know English yet, so Reb Eller taught us in Yiddish," Naftoli reminisces. "He did a fine job. By the time I was enrolled in a proper New York yeshivah, I was at the level for my age, in spite of my tumultuous childhood."

Naftoli remembered the first class he was able to understand in public school was about Arabs and their culture and the food they ate: brown dates sweet as honey, and a highly nutritious, salty, distinctively odorous camel milk. Though he was Jewish, and camel milk was *treif,* he still recalls the satisfaction he had in being able to understand his teacher's words.

His teacher, Mrs. Murphy, a graying, middle-aged kind woman, took a special interest in her student Naftoli.

"Make sure you write me postcards," she told him when he was leaving Oswego for the *yeshivah* in New York. And he did. He wrote her many postcards, utilizing the basic English she had so painstakingly and patiently taught him.

The local Oswego children, unlike their Polish and Hungarian peers who would jeer and taunt the Jews sent like cattle to death, were kind to these shy children. Despite the fact that the newcomers from Europe struggled with the English language, had unusual names and spoke with unusual accents, they didn't make fun of them. They quietly respected the tragic stories their new classmates carried within them, the past that they left behind, and the challenges they were facing in the present.

One memorable Sunday, the committee in charge of the camp brought the refugee children to a movie theatre to see the film *The Lone Ranger*. It was kind of a cultural initiation into the most popular American pastime, movie-going.

Naftoli walked into the movie theater so proud to be one of the crowd carrying a large bag of popcorn. He wasn't a hunted, persecuted subhuman anymore who was denied the right to life, but a free boy in a free country, equal among equals.

After that very special day, every now and then he'd ask Malka and Miriam for money from the small stipend they received each month so he could go to a Sunday movie.

After school, the boys played new games they never heard of before, like baseball and basketball. They played outside until the freezing cold weather of upstate New York, with icy winds blowing from Lake Ontario, set in. During the winter season they learned a new skill, ice skating, a popular sport in the northern part of America. Skating season would last for almost half a year, from as early as the beginning of September, until mid-March.

The Weinstein's took great joy in doing all these fun things, like going to the cinema, playing sports or ice skating, but their dedication to *Yiddishkeit* didn't waver. It was never a question where their allegiance belonged.

"My father was a *chassid*," Naftoli would say. "We knew where we belonged."

CHAPTER SIXTEEN

# *Rising from the Dead*

When they first arrived in Oswego on that warm day in August, they were completely exhausted when they walked into the little apartment they would call home for the next two years. They crashed on to their beds. They must have fallen asleep even before their heads hit their pillows.

When they awoke the next morning, they were informed that there were two separate showers: one for men and one for women. They were instructed to go downstairs to take towels and soap and wait in line for their turn.

Malka took towels for herself and her siblings and went to stand in line. Bored, restless, with so much time to wait and nothing else to do, she leafed through the pile of local newspapers and magazines tucked on a shelf in the hallway. But they were all in English, so she put them aside.

But then, at the bottom of the pile she noticed one magazine written in German, one that she could read, so she started leafing idly through it.

And then, as she turned the page, an announcement leaped at her.

A certain Mrs. Weinstein in Switzerland was looking for her husband and seven children, listing them all by name.

Malka ran her finger down the list.

Was this true? Was this real? *Was this happening?* She could hardly continue to read. Anguished disbelief quickly transformed into breathless euphoria. The list in this newspaper that she just "happened" to see contained *their names!*

They were all listed there, one by one. It was their mother! Alive! She was in Switzerland searching for them!

Malka quickly turned to Miriam, tears streaming down her cheeks, unable to speak, her throat choked with overwhelming emotion and unbelievable relief.

Everything around her was spinning, unreal, like she was in a dreamlike daze.

Unable to utter a word, she showed Miriam the advertisement.

Her tears were gushing out now. Miriam, shocked with awe, leaped into the air and shouted to her younger sisters and brothers, "Mama's alive! MAMA'S ALIVE!!!"

They ran over and Miriam pointed at the ad in the paper.

Malka's proclamation had an absolutely stunning effect. A crowd gathered around the Weinstein children.

"My mother is in Switzerland looking for us!" Miriam held the copy of *Aufbau*, the German-language newspaper published in New York that had somehow made it to Oswego. She waved it in the air so that everyone could look, could see for themselves their names, written black on white, no mistake there.

They were all witness to this miracle. Was it true? Could this really happen? Can loved ones arise from the dead?

It gave hope to everyone in the room, that maybe their loved ones who disappeared into the chaos of war, maybe they were also alive, maybe they also made it out of the Nazi inferno, maybe they were also looking for them, maybe they would also find them one day and be reunited. It *could* happen!

Tears were now streaming down Miriam's cheeks and everyone around them joined in. It was a miracle, no less. They all wanted to hear the story, again and again, to come close to it, to touch it, to be in the presence of this wonder, so that maybe, please G-d, maybe some of this improbable luck would spread and be bestowed on them as well, to hear a name coming to life from the pitch night of oblivion and despair.

Everyone wanted to hear the details and Miriam, usually so shy and quiet, spoke to the enraptured audience and told them the facts of that terrible day when their family had been separated, how their mother and their three little siblings boarded the bus in Modane, France, across the border from Turin, Italy. How the bus had started out and then disappeared into the dust. And they had no idea what had happened to them.

"We were sure," Miriam was whispering through her tears, "they were caught by the Nazis. We mourned them." Everyone in the room was sobbing too. This was everyone's story... seeing their family disappear before their eyes to an unknown destination.

"Before Rome was liberated, on their way out, in retreat, the Nazis swept up anyone, every Jew they could lay a hand on. They caught Papa and put him on a train to the death camps. We have no idea what happened to our father. We have no clue. And now... to discover that Mama is alive... we have no words..."

For the entire Oswego camp it was a celebration, a personal victory for each one of them.

A family reunited.

How they hoped they would be the next ones to tell and retell every one of their own miracles, of finding their loved ones from the midst of Europe's ashes!

<hr />

As soon as she could, Ruth Gruber sent a cable to Switzerland informing Esther that her children were alive and safe in Oswego, New York.

We can only begin to try to imagine the immense emotions Esther felt when she received this message. Her children were alive!

But they could not be reunited. The children were not allowed to leave Oswego, due to their unusual legal status. Brought to the United States on the special Presidential Executive Order, pursuant to deportation back to Europe as soon as the war would be over, they were not full-fledged immigrants. They weren't free to travel around the country. And either way, with the war still raging on that side of the Atlantic, there was no way of sending them to Switzerland or bringing their mother to America.

They were in limbo. They had to wait to be reunited.

But they could comfort themselves with the knowledge that their beloved mother and their youngest siblings Gittele, Avraham Duvid and Meir were alive and comparatively secure, in a neutral country. As long as the Germans were on the losing side of the war, Switzerland was a safe haven.

Their only means of communication was the slow, tedious and unreliable mail, with long waiting times until a letter would reach its destination and another long wait until they would receive a letter back in response.

Bit by bit the Weinstein children learned what actually happened from the time their mother and their three youngest siblings boarded that fateful bus.

The bus never crossed the border to Italy. As they approached the Italian border, the driver saw the German roadblocks in the distance. Acting decisively, he quickly turned off the main road and rattled onto the dirt road, going south, looking for a loophole to sneak across the border.

But the border was sealed. Italy was overrun by Germans. Instead, he drove two hundred and seventy miles, all the way to southern France, to the Mediterranean coastal city of Nice, to a safe house.

Not all the buses were so fortunate. Some were intercepted, driving straight into the checkpoints set up by the Germans. Their passengers ended up in Auschwitz.

Thanks to the ingenuity and courage of their bus driver, Esther and her three little ones found themselves in Nice. There they were greeted by a young girl with an unassuming, bespectacled face, Marianne Cohn, a legend in the Resistance world, who had only recently been released from Nazi prison.

Marianne grew up in a secular intellectual Jewish family in Mannheim, Germany. With the rise of Nazism, the Cohns moved to Spain and in 1938 relocated to France. When France was occupied by the Nazis, her parents were arrested and deported to Gurs Internment Camp as German nationals. She and her sister were smuggled to a farm run by a Jewish Scouts Organization, where she discovered her Jewish roots.

In 1942, when she was twenty years old, Marianne began working for the OSE (Œuvre de Secours aux Enfants), smuggling Jewish children out of Nazi controlled territories. A year later, in 1943, she was arrested but miraculously released after three months of intensive interrogations.

During that incarceration she wrote a poem that would later become a manifesto of those days, "Je trahirai demain" (I shall betray tomorrow). Her poem began with these stark, haunting words:

Tomorrow, I shall betray, not today.
Today, tear out my fingernails.
I shall not betray.
You don't know how long I can hold out
But I know.

The torture didn't deter Marianne. As soon as she was released, she returned to shuttling out of France two to three groups a month of up to twenty-five to thirty children. This is when Esther met her.

From Nice, Marianne led Esther, Gittele, Avraham Duvid, Meir, and a dozen or so more, to Lyon, continuing up north to Chapelle-des-Bois, a tiny village hidden in the Jura Mountains of Vallée de Joux, on the Swiss border. There, in relative obscurity, they waited for their turn to cross the border. Marianne handed the group over to the *passeurs* – the locals who lived in adjacent hamlets hugging the Franco-Swiss border.

Tragically, a year later, on May 31, 1944, during one of these runs, Marianne Cohn was arrested by the Germans in the northern French town Annemasse, near the Swiss border. As she was held in prison for over a month, in her last letter, awaiting her ultimate fate, she wrote that she feared that children would be taken to Drancy or to a concentration camp. She also wrote that she wasn't allowed to have her prayer book with her.

A rescue operation was planned to have her extracted from prison, with active help from the Mayor of Annemasse, Jan Deffaugt (who was recognized by Yad Vashem in 1966 as one of the Righteous Among the Gentiles), but Marianne Cohn refused, fearing that there would be reprisals on the children she felt responsible for, that they would be endangered by the intervention for her. On July 8, 1944 she was taken to the nearby forest, brutally tortured and bludgeoned to death by French militiamen.

Her haunting poem would ultimately become the story of her life.

The twenty-eight children that she accompanied on that fateful last journey, would survive the war, as Esther, Gittele, Avraham Duvid, and Meir did the year before.

May the memory of Marianne Cohn, a fearless Jewish soul, be blessed.

In mid-1943, Esther and the three little ones were hiding in a French village, deep in the mountains of Vallée de Joux, in the heart of the Risoux Forest, waiting to cross the border into Switzerland. The people she entrusted her life with, these *passeurs*, were a tiny secretive group of local villagers.

These fifteen young men and women included some professional smugglers doing it for money, while others, members of the Resistance, were recruited in 1940 by the Swiss Information Service, which was part of the Swiss Intelligence. Born in this frontier area, frequently with their front door in Switzerland and their backyard in France, they knew every trail and hidden pathway in the Grand Risoux forest.

They set up a small group of *passeurs* to organize, supervise and guide safe passage along up to two hundred kilometers of forest trails in Risoux Forest Massif. Not only were people, fighters and refugees, transported across the border. Confidential documents recorded on microfilm regarding Nazi movements were smuggled to the British

Embassy in Lausanne, alongside armaments to resistance fighters over the border back in France.

In those desperate times, instead of hiding in their daily lives and minding their own business, sheltered from calamities of the outside world, the *passeurs* chose to take sides. "Do something against the Germans," as Bernard Bouveret, the last surviving *passeur* put it.

If encountered by German patrols during daytime, their documents and belongings would be inspected. At night, they would be shot on sight. If captured, they were inevitably deported to concentration camps such as Dachau.

Esther and her children would never forget the pure kindness of the two *passeurs*, Anne-Marie Piguet and Victoria Cordier, the young girls who dedicated themselves exclusively to smuggling Jewish children to Switzerland, saving lives, one life at a time.

The trails were very difficult to access. On top of the geographically challenging terrain, the smugglers were playing cat and mouse with the German patrols that were making great efforts to seal the border by ambushing the trails. On an almost daily basis the *passeurs* would alternate the route and find new pathways and detours to avoid getting caught. Due to the difficulty of the task, the *passeurs* could take only very few on every passage.

They started with Gittele.

After the exhausting trek across the forest, the *passeurs* left her in Le Rendezvous des Sages, a tiny wooden hut deep in the forest, on the Swiss side of the border. A little girl, she couldn't understand why she was separated from her family. Feeling lonely and scared, she didn't stop crying for another two days, until her brother Avraham Duvid arrived. Esther arrived last with Meir.

From the hideout they were transferred to Geneva, claimed refugee status, and were placed in a family internment camp. They would stay there for more than three years, until November 13, 1946.

Meir grew up hearing the story of their escape that contained sketchy details he couldn't quite put together. The gist of it was that at some point Meir was separated from his mother and siblings and the family that sheltered him did not want to give him back. The person caring for him denied that he was Esther's child. To finally reunite him with his family, it took someone else who looked at Meir, looked at Esther, and said, "Can't you see the resemblance? She's definitely the mother."

The unflattering truth of Swiss policies toward the refugees and the realities of the day-to-day life of Jewish survivors of Nazi persecution on Swiss soil during the war remains a dark page in history books, obscured by big money and big politics.

Ever since World War II, Switzerland maintained that it had no other option but to observe strictly neutral status, otherwise it would be inexorably overrun by Germany. Its policies were those of walking the tightrope of bare necessity, trying behind the scenes to help the Allies and at the same time avoid direct confrontation with Germany and thus inflict even more suffering on those who took shelter in the country.

However, the facts were different.

After 1938, when the Nazi party was already reigning supreme in Germany and the persecution against the Jews was escalating, Swiss refugee policy toward the mainly Jewish refugees was a direct continuation of the anti-Jewish policy of the interwar years. It remained uncompromising. It was not, as is often maintained, primarily a reaction to the difficult political, material, and military situation of small, neutral Switzerland at the time, but an inherent policy line of Switzerland, consistent with its historical and political imperative of isolationism.

It was a Swiss diplomatic initiative in Berlin that led to the use of "J" in the passports of German and Austrian Jews. This enabled Swiss border authorities to single them out and deny them entry.

The border was sealed on two especially momentous occasions: in 1938, when Austrian Jews tried to escape after the Anschluss of Austria to the German Reich, and in 1942–1943, when the Jews of France, Belgium, and Holland were being deported to the death camps in Poland. The Swiss authorities sealed the borders to thousands of refugees despite having full knowledge of the dire fate that was awaiting these people seeking refuge.

In the summer of 1942, this policy sparked public unrest and a heated debate in parliament, but nothing changed. An estimated twenty-four thousand Jewish refugees were either rejected at the border or sent back to their countries from 1938 to 1944, the majority in the critical period of 1942–1943. The overwhelming majority of them perished. Callous deletion of history continued even after the war as most of the relevant files were destroyed in the 1950s. Therefore, neither the exact fate of those denied entry, nor the exact number of victims is known, and never will be.

Nevertheless, twenty two thousand and five hundred Jewish refugees managed to get into Switzerland from 1938 to 1944. According to the 1931–1933 Law they were all supposed to "transmigrate," that is, leave Switzerland as soon as they could arrange passage to some third country, usually overseas.

With France's occupation in 1940, however, this became nearly impossible, as Switzerland found itself encircled by the Nazis from all sides. Esther and her three children were among the fortunate ones who were smuggled over the border into the country, succeeding in evading Swiss border patrols and reporting to immigration agencies.

In 1940 the Swiss government decided to intern most of the refugees who were unable to leave. But the authorities didn't treat them kindly. First the men were put in labor camps and from 1942, women, younger children, and the elderly were sent to "homes." These were mainly old houses, unused hotels, or vacation compounds where the people lived and worked under slightly better conditions than the men in the labor camps.

Many of the more than twenty-two thousand Jewish refugees in Switzerland were kept in unheated barracks and forced to sleep on straw. Men were put to work in fields, forests and factories while women and girls cleaned homes of Swiss officials.

This was not simply an oversight, or an expediency of harsh times. It was a premeditated policy, formulated by Dr. Heinrich Rothmond, a Swiss Ministry of Justice and Police official during the war who stated, "'Let them huddle on their straw as long as possible, so that, of themselves, they will be led to ask permission to leave. Let them see for themselves that Switzerland is no paradise so that those who want to come in will be discouraged."

As the Schom-Wiesenthal report states, older children were distributed among Swiss families. Families were often separated for years.

This particular detail is the harrowing historical background to Meir's fragmentary memory. He must have been separated from his mother and two other siblings and placed with a Swiss family, while his mother was sent to a "home" where she was forced to work in severe conditions.

After the war was over and she was forced to "transmigrate," meaning leave Switzerland at the first opportunity, she of course came looking for her son, but the adoptive family attempted to deny them the chance of reuniting. Thank G-d for the honest person, whoever he or she was, who called Meir's surrogate family's bluff, and thereby helped Esther retrieve her son.

It was when Esther was working at the internment home that she placed an ad in the Swiss paper, searching for her husband and children. She knew that when she left Modane, attempting to cross the border to Italy, the rest of her family was attempting to do the same. And she knew that there were only two possibilities of what could have happened to them. They were captured by the Germans and immediately deported to their deaths... or maybe, maybe, hopefully, they had evaded capture and made their way to Switzerland just like she did.

On the faint, dim hope that maybe somehow, somewhere, they were still alive, she had to try to find them. She wrote the words for the ad, with a prayer in her heart. She never considered putting an ad in an American paper.

A German Jew living in Washington, DC, often bought newspapers and magazines from Zurich. It was he that read Esther's ad searching for her children.

It was he that decided, on a whim, to place an ad in the *Aufbau*, the American German magazine, hoping that by sheer coincidence a Jew who knew German and who happened to read this issue of the magazine and stumbled upon this ad would know something or someone that might be of help. It was like throwing a dart into a barn full of hay and hoping that it would hit the needle buried there. But sometimes, if *hashgacha protis* has its way, this is exactly what happens.

One person can take a step that can change the course of events, sometimes changing the life of one person, or an entire family. Once in a while, without knowing it, we become vessels for Divine Providence and connect loose ends in this world of infinite odds. A random person decides to post Esther's ad in an American German newspaper? And Malka sees this ad?

The Oswego officials reached out to the Red Cross in Switzerland and a representative found Esther Weinstein. Imagine that day when he told her the news that she was not alone with three young children in this world. That Malka, Miriam, Berel, Leah, Yankel, and Naftoli were alive and well in America, waiting to reunite with her.

The newspaper, *Aufbau*, published an article about how its list of refugees had led to the family's reunion. When the man who put in this ad read the story in the newspaper and learned that his ad had reunited the Weinstein's, he was beyond ecstatic. He immediately wrote Malka a long letter expressing his joy and requesting that they send him photos of her family – his new family!

Malka of course sent pictures and a deep, heartfelt letter of thanks. They corresponded for years after this momentous event.

As the war drew to a close, the refugees in Oswego were filled with anxiety. Nobody wanted to return to blood soaked Europe. Pro-Jewish organizations lobbied endlessly to procure citizenship for the *Haven* refugees. First lady Eleanor Roosevelt, who visited the refugee camp with Henry Morgenthau, tried to pressure her husband to fast track them to citizenship, but he was adamant that they be sent back. His death on April 12, 1945, less than a month before May 8, V-Day, changed everything.

Harry Truman, the new President hastily sworn-in after the death of FDR, was swamped by the havoc of the last days of war, by a world drowning in a post-war chaos, imperiled by another menace rising from the East. The Soviet Union was attempting to hijack Europe just as it was liberated from the Nazis, to claim its share of the new world order.

It took Harry Truman a long eight months to clean the table and turn his attention to this comparatively obscure issue of the *Haven* refugees. At last he granted them the path to citizenship, thus revoking the precondition of the Executive Order issued by his predecessor that restricted their residence in the United States for only the duration of hostilities.

On December 22, 1946, the soon-to-be citizens were bused to the Canadian side of the Niagara Falls in Ontario where they were granted an immigrant status and re-entered the United States across the Rainbow Bridge. On their own feet, they walked into a country they could now call their new home.

Cousins in Williamsburg that they'd never met, the Goldfischer family, discovered they were in America when they read the article printed about them searching for their mother. The Goldfischer's contacted them and when the Weinstein's left Oswego, they took the children under their wing, inviting them to come and stay with them until they would find a more permanent place to live.

Malka and Miriam found work in a factory that helped pay the rent and support them. Naftoli and Yankel were accepted on a full scholarship into a Lubavitch Yeshivah, living with a kind Jewish family. Berel received a full scholarship, along with room and board, in the Yeshivah Tifereth Yerushalayim, and Leah received a full scholarship to Bais Yaakov of Williamsburg.

During one of Naftoli's first days in *yeshivah*, he saw a teacher who looked so much like his father that his breath caught in his throat, his heart thumping in excitement before he burst into a rush of tears. He ran to the bathroom to pour out his heart, sobbing endless tears. It was not uncommon for those with broken hearts and crushed hopes to cry unabated. They still had no idea for sure whether their father was alive, what had happened to him, and here was a teacher who looked just like his father!

It was a searing, anguished pain to think that they had lost their courageous father who had done the impossible, navigating the high, stormy seas of war-ravaged Europe. And at almost the very end he fell in the battle of rescuing his family.

If they could so miraculously discover that their mother and siblings were still alive, maybe their father was too, somewhere, somehow.

They had a mother and they had their siblings, all of them, alive. How could they even put into words what this meant to them? They had a knowledge that changed the way they felt about this world, about themselves.

# Epilogue:

It would take three more years before they were reunited with their mother and their siblings Gittele, Avraham Duvid and Meir.

Esther worked in an internment home in Geneva until the end of the war, and then moved to Clarence, to a family camp, until November of 1946. Her daughter Sarah and her family had also miraculously survived the war and lived in Antwerp. As soon as there was a physical possibility to do so, they moved to Antwerp, and lived with her daughter Sarah Sussholz and her family.

Finally, in 1948, they received entry visas to America and sailed on a ship across the Atlantic.

Malka, Miriam, Berel, Leah, Yankel and Naftoli all came to the port to meet the ship as it came into the harbor. They were all there to see their mother, Gittele, Avraham Duvid and Meir for the first time in five years.

It was an emotional reunion that defied description, marred only by the fact that their father Chaim Yair was not with them and they would never see him again. The last witness to see Chaim Yair alive in Aushchwitz was on the 9th of Kislev and it would forever be the date his family commemorated his yahrzeit.

It didn't matter to them that the apartment in Williamsburg that was allocated to them by The Joint was small and did not have heated water. After all those years separated, not knowing what would be, they didn't need much to feel the rays of light and happiness.

They were reunited together again.

The Weinstein family left Antwerp, Belgium, and traveled to France, where they spent different periods of times in Montesquieu, Aix-les-Bains, Agde, Nantes-en-Ratier, Colombières, and Modane. Eventually, Chaim Yair, Sarah, Malka, Miriam, Berel, Leah, Yankel, and Naftoli wound up in Italy, where they lived in Turin, Milan, Florence, and Rome. Chaim Yair was sent to Auschwitz, where he was murdered by the Nazis.

Esther Weinstein was with her husband and children from Antwerp, Belgium, up to Modane, France. Then she and the younger children – Gittele, Avraham Duvid, and Meir – went to Nice, France, and in due course to Switzerland. Esther, Malka, Miriam, Berel, Leah, Yankel, Naftoli, Gittele, Avraham Duvid, and Meir finally reunited in America. Sarah went back to Antwerp.

APPENDIX I

# *Sources*

Sources that provided the historical background for information used to help write this memoir include:

INTERVIEWS WITH FAMILY MEMBERS
1. Malka Greenzweig on May 1, 2018.
2. R' Naftoli Weinstein on May 4, 2018.
3. Meir Weinstein on May 24, 2018.
4. Jacqui Sussholz on June 4, 2018.
5. Alexandre Speaker on May 25, 2018.
6. Baruch Katz on December 14, 2018.
7. Estee Shakovsky, on October 25, 2018.
8. David Sussholz's historical video.
9. Frieda Sussholz's unpublished memoir.

WEBSITES
1. https://encyclopedia.ushmm.org/ (United States Holocaust Memorial Museum Encyclopedia
2. yadvashem.org
3. ort.org.

ARTICLES
1. Article in Belzer magazine, *Ohr Hatzofon*.
2. *Barbed Wire Haven*, Michal Eisikowitz, *Mishpacha*, June, 2013.
3. Guardian magazine:https://www.theguardian.com/world/2010/oct/03/marshal-petain-nazi-zealous-anti-semitism, *Disclosed: The Zealous Way Marshal Pétain Enforced Nazi anti-Semitic Laws*

4. New York Times https://www.nytimes.com/1998/01/15/world/jews-remember-forced-labor-camps-in-wartime-swiss-refuge.html

DOCUMENTARY
1. *The Jews Who Fled the Holocaust Over the Pyrenees*, Gustau Nerín.

BOOKS:
1. *Jews in France During World War II*, Renée Poznanski, p. 386–8.
2. *The United States Holocaust Memorial Museum Encyclopedia of Camps and Ghettos*, edited by Geoffrey P. Megargee, Joseph R. White.
3. *Triumph of Survival: The Story of the Jews in the Modern Era 1650–1990*, Berel Wein.
4. *Père Marie-Benoît and Jewish Rescue*, Susan Zuccotti.
5. *The Italians and the Holocaust: Persecution, Rescue, and Survival*, Susan Zuccotti.
6. *Haven: The Dramatic Story of 1,000 World War II Refugees and How They Came to America*, Ruth Gruber.

# APPENDIX II
## Documents

*Belz magazine, Ohr Hatzofon, featured this article about Rabbi Chaim Yair Weinstein, c. 2008, translation found on page 227*

## Hidden Children in France

**Searching for Surname (phonetically like) : WEINSTEIN**
**12 matching records found.**
Run on Thu, 06 Dec 2018 09:11:24 -0700

| Name | Date of Birth / Place of Birth | Nationality | Place | Page | Comments |
|---|---|---|---|---|---|
| WEINSTEIN, Jacques | | | 22-Nov-41 | 128 | |
| WEINSTEIN, Jacques | 20-May-1934 | Czechoslovak | Creuse-Chateau de Masgelier Feb 1941 | 117 | |
| WEINSTEIN, Jacques | 30-May-1934 | Czechoslovak | Creuse-Chateau de Masgelier Feb 1941 | 115 | |
| WEINSTEIN, Jacques | 30-May-1934 / Anvers | Czechoslovak | Creuse-Chateau de Masgelier March 1941 | 125 | |
| WEINSTEIN, Jacques | 7 years old | | Creuse-Chateau de Masgelier Nov Dec 1941 | 119 | |
| WEINSTEIN, Jacques | 30-May-1934 / Anvers | Czechoslovak | Creuse-Chateau du Masgelier Jan 1942 | 93 | |
| WEINSTEIN, Lea | | | 22-Nov-41 | 128 | |
| WEINSTEIN, Lea | 01-Aug-1932 | Czechoslovak | Creuse-Chateau de Masgelier Feb 1941 | 115 | |
| WEINSTEIN, Lea | 01-Aug-1932 | Czechoslovak | Creuse-Chateau de Masgelier Feb 1941 | 117 | |
| WEINSTEIN, Lea | 01-Aug-1932 / Anvers | Czechoslovak | Creuse-Chateau de Masgelier March 1941 | 125 | |

| Name | Date of Birth / Place of Birth | Nationality | Place | Page | Comments |
|---|---|---|---|---|---|
| WEINSTEIN, Lea | 9 years old | | Creuse-Chateau de Masgelier Nov Dec 1941 | 119 | |
| WEINSTEIN, Lea | 01-Aug-1932 / Anvers | Czechoslovak | Creuse-Chateau du Masgelier Jan 1942 | 93 | |

*Database of the Weinstein children hidden in France, including Jacques and Lea (aka Yankel and Leah) who were in the Chateau du Masgelier, February 1941*

*Article in the Morgen, August 9, 1944, describing the Weinstein family's desperate search for their mother. Translation found on page 229*

*Two articles printed in the Aufbau, August 11, 1944 and December 22, 1944, describing how the list of names in the German newspaper led to the reunion of the Weinstein children with their mother and three siblings. Translations follow on page 233*

*Excerpts from an article about Miriam Weinstein that appeared in the The Jewish Voice, Sep. 1944. Translation found on page 232*

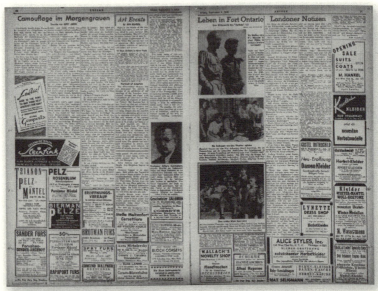

*The Weinstein children in Oswego, New York, eating their first American ice cream, Aufbau, 1944*

*List of the Weinstein siblings in Oswego, New York, unknown source*

12/6/2018      Jewish Arrivals In Switzerland 1938 - 1945

An affiliate of the Museum of Jewish Heritage – A Living Memorial to the Holocaust

Logged in: Boruch Katz
My Profile | Logout

powered by ancestry.com

Home » Databases » Jewish Arrivals In Switzerland 1938 - 1945

## Jewish Arrivals In Switzerland 1938 - 1945

Searching for Surname (phonetically like) : WEINSTEIN
7 matching records found.
Run on Thu, 06 Dec 2018 09:13:13 -0700

| Name (Maiden Name) | Gender / Date of Birth | Arrival Date | Nationality I / Nationality II | Comments |
|---|---|---|---|---|
| WEINSTEIN, Alfred | M / 31-Dec-1925 | 21-Dec-1942 | Deutschland / Staatenlos | |
| WEINSTEIN, Bertha | F / 13-May-1937 | 26-Oct-1943 | Tschechoslowakei / Tschechoslowakei | |
| WEINSTEIN, Esther | F / 28-Feb-1900 | 26-Oct-1943 | Tschechoslowakei / Tschechoslowakei | |
| WEINSTEIN, Frieda | F / 08-Mar-1927 | 19-Nov-1943 | Belgien / Belgien | |
| WEINSTEIN, Jakob | M / 05-Aug-1892 | 23-Nov-1943 | Jugoslawien / Jugoslawien | |
| WEINSTEIN, Michel | M / 04-Mar-1943 | 26-Oct-1943 | Tschechoslowakei / Tschechoslowakei | |
| WEINSTEIN, Robert | M / 13-Jul-1939 | 26-Oct-1943 | Tschechoslowakei / Tschechoslowakei | |

*Database of Jewish arrivals in Switzerland, including Esther Weinstein and three of her children, Bertha, Robert and Michel (Gitel, Avraham Duvid and Meir)*

**Merkos L'Inyonei Chinuch, Inc.**
770 EASTERN PARKWAY
BROOKLYN, N. Y.

מרכז
לעניני חנוך
770 איסטערן פארקוויי.
ברוקלין, נ. י.

RABBI JOSEPH I. SCHNEERSOHN,
President

Chairman, Exec. Committee
RABBI MENDEL SCHNEERSON

Director
RABBI M. A. HODAKOV

Executive Secretary
NISSAN J. MINDEL, M.A.

ב"ה יום ב' ב' אלול ח'תש"ד

ב"ק אדמו"ר שליט"א מליובאוויטש.
נשיא

יו"ר ועד הפועל:
הרב מנחם מ. שניאורסאהן

מנהל:
הרב מ. א. חדקוב

מזכיר ראשי:
ניסן י. מינדל

כבוד ידיד"נו הרב הנכבד והנעלה אי"א וו"ח
כו' וכו' מהרמ"י שי' צעקאוואל

שלום וברכה !

שלחנו לבה"ר סדור עשטם תורה אור, חמשים ספרי תהלים וארבעה
כרכים משניות (2 סט ש"ס).

באם נחוצים עוד ספרי תהלים נא להודיענו ונשלח להם אי"ה.

ונא יחזק כעת ביותר את ועד החרדים בכלל ואת מר ראמשלד שי'
בפרט שיסדרו את אמירת תהלים בצבור אחר תפלת שחרית ולפי דברי
מר ראמשלד שי' בטח יובלו כעת לסדר גם השעור של משניות,

מעונינים אנו לדעת ממהלך העבודה של הועד, למסכות שבח" לנערות
ע"ד בתי הספר לנערות, "בית רבקה", בית שרה" וע"ד השעורים למדריכות
שבהנהלת זוגות הרבנים הנכבדה חא"י, גם ע"י שעות העבודה בדי שנוכל
לקבוע התקציב.

במה הגיע כבר לידי בתה"ר שתי החבילות של ספרים וחוברות אשר
"מחנה ישראל" והמל"ח י"י שלחו לו בשבוע העבר, ואמר סדנינו שוב
בדבר החוסר לקריאת מוצאי"ש אנו לנכון שלא לחלק הספרים חנ"ל ולחפיצם
סתם, אלא ליסד "בית קריאה" הפתוחה בשעות קבועות לכל הרוצה לבוא שמה
ולקרוא הספרים והחוברות שם גופא או לקחתם משם ע"מ להחזירם
כעבר זמן.

ובאם כתה"ר יסכים בכלל להצעתנו זו, נא למסור לזוגתו הרבנית תחי'
את בקשתנו לסנות את אחת הנערות למנהלת "בית הקריאה" בשכר ארבע או
חמשה לשבוע, ואשר היא תשגיח על הומר הקריאה ותרשום את האנשים

*Letter from the Rebbe Rayatz to Rabbi Tzebovol, mentioning the Shabbos parties Malka and Miriam Weinstein helped organize in Oswego, New York, 1944. Translation follows on page 234*

> RABBI J. SCHNEERSOHN
> OF LUBAWITZ
> 770 EASTERN PARKWAY
> BROOKLYN 13, N. Y.
> SLOCUM 6-2919

> יוסף יצחק שניאורסאהן
> ליובאוויטש

> ב"ה, כ"ז אלול, תש"ד
> ברוקלין

> אל הרבנית מרת רבקה מינדעל תחי'
> הנשיאה של ועד מסיבות שבת במחנה
> אסוועגא, וסגנותי' מבחירות מרת מלכה
> תחי' וויינשטיין, מרת מרים תחי'
> וויינשטיין, מרת ניזל החי' זיגעלמאן
> ומרת מוה החי' דרעזנער.
> ה' עליהן יחיו.

> שלום וברכה!

> בזה הנני לברך אתהן ואת הוריהן ובני ביתם
> יחיו, בברכת כתיבה וחתימה טובה לשנה טובה ומתוקה
> בגשמיות וברוחניות.
> נהניתי לשמוע מאשר לקחו על עצמן את עניני
> ההדרכה בחנוך הכשר ולסדר בעזה"י את המסבות שבת,
> התחזקו לפעול ולעשות כמדת הראוי וברכות ימולו על
> ראשיכן.
> המברכן

*Letter from the Rebbe Rayatz to Malka and Miriam Weinstein, acknowledging their contribution to the Shabbos parties they helped organize in Oswego, New York, 1944. Translation follows on page 235*

```
The following girls have been granted full scholarships by the
Beth Jacob School of Boro Park, 1413 - 45th Street, Brooklyn, N. Y.,
which includes room and board:

    Franco, Rachel          age 11
    Krantz, Edita                9
    Gal, Charlotte               9
    Merzer, Yvonne              12
    Strika, Gertrude            10
    Blaustein, Susannah         11

The following girls have been granted full scholarships by the
Beth Yaakov of Williamsburg, 255 Division Avenue, Brooklyn, N. Y.,
which includes room and board:

    Buchler, Blanca
    Weinstein, Laya
```

*Scholarship recipients, including Laya (Leah) Weinstein, date unknown*

```
The following pupils have been granted full scholarships by the Mesifta
Tifereth Jerusholaim, 145 E. Broadway, New York City, which includes room
and board:

    Dresner, Abraham        age 16
        "   Isadore             15
        "   Rudolphe            14
        "   Solomon            12½
        "   Joseph              9½
    Weinstein, Bernard          16
        "   Jack               11½
        "   Nathan              9½
    Krauthamer, Simon          13½
        "   Jules               12

The following pupils have been granted full scholarships by the Mesifta
Torah Vodaath, 141 So. 3rd Street, Brooklyn, N. Y., which includes room and
board:

    Seigelman, Andre             9
    Franco, David                7
    Wolken, Rene                12
    Buchler, Moshe Shimon       11
```

*Scholarship recipients, including Bernard, Jack and Nathan (Berel, Yankel and Naftoli) Weinstein, date unknown*

Photo of a listing in a book of those who perished in Auschwitz. This may be Chaim Yair Weinstein of Munkacs, Czechoslovakia, Auschwitz archives

> 2-23-1945
>
> I can give a table from my office for the family Weinstein, with the authorisation of the administration.
>
> Rabbi M. Tzechoval

*Rabbi M. Tzchechwall's offer to give one of his tables to the Weinstein family, Oswego, New York, February 23, 1945*

*Letter to Rabbi Moshe Tzebovol that mentions when Dovid Sussholz was attacked and almost killed by burglars. Translation follows on page 236*

APPENDIX III

# Translation of Documents

---

Translation of article about Rabbi Chaim Yair Weinstein, printed in the Belz magazine, Ohr Hatzofon, c. 2008

## HARAV HACHOSSID REB CHAIM YAIR WEINSTEIN

Harav HaChossid Reb Chaim Yair Hacohen Weinstein *z"l* was an example of a fiery Chossid, a truthful man, straight and reliable, who did not favor anyone. He dealt with all matters that came up with *kovoid shomayim* in mind, and when there was a need, he was not afraid to zealously stand up for Hashem's name.

He originated from Munkatch, Hungary, and when Reb Yisochor Dov from Belz *zy"a* settled in Ratsferd after World War 1, Reb Chaim Yair traveled there to see the Tsaddik, and from then connected to the Tsaddikim of Belz with his whole heart and soul.

Reb Chaim Yair was a devoted Chossid, and after he got married, he traveled to Belz to dwell in the Rebbe's shade and to warm up in the atmosphere of the "Yoshvim." He stayed there for three years, learning Torah and Chassidus with fervor, rising in spiritual greatness, and forgetting about the entire world, customary to the great "Yoshvim."

In 1921, he arrived in Antwerp with his family to serve as a shochet, but for various reasons the position didn't work out, so he was appointed the head mashgiach over all the butchers – twenty in total! – in Antwerp. He also owned a fruit store, which provided him with a living.

In the history books of Antwerp, it says that Reb Chaim Yair made massive changes in the chain of butchers, solved important problems, despite opposition from certain people, especially the local butchers, who obviously weren't particularly excited about these changes. Even when he wanted to stop with that holy work, since he made enough of a living from his fruit store, he asked Reb Aharon of Belz *zy"a* for his permission and was told to keep the position.

The rebbe's holy command kept up his spirit, and Reb Chaim Yair, who was strengthened with the passion of Belz not to be embarrassed of being mocked, fulfilled his job with great strength, fearless of everyone and ignoring personal interests, his only ambition to keep up the standard of Yiddishkeit.

As a loyal Chossid he traveled on a few occasions from Antwerp to spend time near the rebbe. He excelled in Chassidus his entire life and always strived to reach the level of a true *oived Hashem* with a full heart.

During World War II, he wandered from place to place until he reached Italy, which he thought to be his refuge. But two weeks before the liberation of Rome by the Allied forces, he was caught and sent to Auschwitz, while his whole family survived.

May Hashem avenge his blood.

Translation of the article in the Morgen describing the Weinstein family's desperate search for their mother.

## FOURTEEN-YEAR-OLD JEWISH BOY RELATES HOW NAZIS HAVE TORN AWAY HIS FATHER.

*By M.Y. Nirenberger*

Oswego, New York, Tuesday. The Jewish refugees, who have made it here, are the first witnesses to the terrible and scary tragedy of the European Jewry. They have seen with their own eyes how the Nazis harassed Jews – many of them have felt the Nazis' murderous lashes on their own skin, have been through the biggest distresses and sufferings, and have witnessed how other Jews have been massacred in the Nazi countries. Those Jewish refugees whom America has brought to the refugee camp of Fort Ontario are the living witnesses of our Jewish holocaust, and they have asked me to pass on to the readers of the *Morgen* their endurance. "The world should know of our suffering in Europe," one of them told me. "You should make sure that the maximum amount of people should know about it, because I'm under the impression that many of them here don't believe the full truth about the Jewish holocaust in Europe and therefore don't realize the importance of evacuating the remains of the Jewish nation in Nazi-Europe."

*Lost their father and mother on the way*
The horrifying story of the Weinstein family has left the most terrible impression on me during my visit to that local refugee town. The Weinsteins are a family of six, with missing parents – the parents have been torn away by the Nazis. When I arrived at Fort Ontario, I encountered a little boy who looked like he was about ten or eleven years old, but he is so small and skinny as a result of his sufferings; he is, in fact, fourteen years old. Bernard Weinstein is a very intelligent young man, also a very religious one. He doesn't know any English, so could therefore only very poorly communicate with the local

Americans who had wanted to talk to him. He has very clear and intelligent eyes, an intelligent face, and a lot of people have tried talking to him. The first question that troubled him was whether I speak French or not, and when I told him that I do, he was delighted. A while later, he told me that he is from Antwerp, where his father was a *mashgiach*. Suddenly, after telling me his father was a kosher-meat *mashgiach*, it occurred to me that he must speak Yiddish. "Do you speak Yiddish?" I asked him. "For sure," he answered in a melodious Polish-Galician accent. And he started relating to me the following:

"My parents escaped Antwerp as the invasion began, and they took all ten of us children with them. We wandered around Belgium, then around France until we arrived in Italy. My father originated from Košice, Czechoslovakia, and my mother from the little village Checovic, near Košice. I went to the Yesode Hatorah Yeshiva in Antwerp where I received a strictly religious upbringing, just like all of us children did. By the way, I would indeed like to ask you, since I have no *Tefillin* and *Talit katan*, you should try and make sure I get them."

That's how he spoke muddling different subjects, and when I calmed him down assuring him that in America he will receive a pair of *Tefillin*, he continued telling me about the tale of their wanderings. Then a little girl joined us, whom he introduced to me: "That's my ten-year-old sister Leah." Leah asked me if I could tell her whether her mother who got lost on the way, and her father whom the Nazis dragged away, can be found. I tried comforting her, but her sharp Jewish eyes remained skeptical.... She burst out crying... and Bernard Weinstein carried on with his story.

"After lengthy wanderings, we arrived in southern France, near Marseille, but the Nazis were chasing us. We fled to Grenoble, then to [text cut out, first page, bottom of middle column] which was under Italian control, where Jews were also put in camps, but were not tortured like under the Germans. As long as the Italians were in control, it was not too bad in that area. We stayed in the village of Saint-Gervais where the situation was sustainable, taking the circumstances into account. But – that was as long as the Germans didn't chase away the Italians. About a year after Mussolini was no longer in charge, and the Nazis took control over the area, the Jews started being persecuted again. A few Italian officers told us that they will help us save ourselves because the Nazis had started deporting the Jews to Poland. They helped us enter Italy. But – not all of us, they couldn't take our mother; she was ill. She stayed behind with the Germans with a little child, begging us to go with the Italians.... She was crying, understanding that we would have rather stayed behind with her, but she didn't want to hear about us staying... We left, and that's how I, my sister Malka (nineteen years old), my sister Miriam (eighteen years old), my brother Jack (ten years old), and my brother Nathan (eight years old) all saved our lives. Also my married sister and another brother who is in Rome saved themselves.

"The Nazis continued chasing us; they also arrived in Rome and started hunting Jews. They were hunting Jews in the streets, just like animals are hunted. They managed to capture thousands of Jews. I don't know how many unfortunate ones fell prey to their hands. We children hid ourselves with Christians. They hid us and that's how we were saved.

"But what resulted from that for us..." (Here, Bernard Weinstein couldn't control himself anymore and burst out crying.) "My totty, my good father, has been captured and deported by the Nazis." While Bernard Weinstein was recounting his dreadful experiences, his sisters joined him. Seeing their brother crying, the sisters started crying too. I tried calming down the little unfortunate Bernard, but he would not let himself be comforted. I realized that there was no point in me trying to calm him down, he wasn't crying like a child that can be comforted with a little snack, but like an embittered unfortunate Jew.

I don't know the names of my relatives in New York, he told me. I know we have relatives here, and if they'll read your article I ask them to come and talk to us. When I was already quite far away, he shouted after me, "Don't forget about the *Tefillin*!" I promised him, and through the *Morgen* fulfilled his request.

**Translation of an article about Miriam Weinstein that appeared in the Jewish Voice, September 1944**

Miriam (Marcel) Weinstein represents the tragedy of a family torn apart. She, that young child (about eighteen years old), is the mother to three little brothers and two little sisters. It's impossible to describe the difficult wanderings of the group of children from Munkacs, Czechoslovakia, Belgium, France, Italy, to Fort Ontario. A father and mother do not abandon their children so quickly! She doesn't know anyone here. Maybe some men from Munkacs who know their parents will appear? That's already a gloomy and doubtful request!... Where are the parents? Only one great G-d knows!...

Translation of two articles printed in the Aufbau, August 11, 1944 and December 22, 1944, describing how the list of names in the German newspaper led to the reunion of the Weinstein children with their mother and three siblings.

## FOUND!

The first joyful surprise that the six orphan children, the Weinstein siblings from Czechoslovakia, received after their arrival at Fort Ontario, was the news that their mother is alive. The eldest of the children, nineteen-year-old Marcella (Malka) Weinstein, discovered the name of her mother while flipping through the pages of an edition of the *Aufbau* in a list of the Jews who fled from France to Switzerland, from whom the children had been separated for years and about whom had not heard anything. After the collapse of France, as thousands of refugees fled the Nazis in all directions, the children, who are now between the ages of nine and nineteen, lost their parents. The children had then managed to escape to Italy, from where they were brought to America. They heard that their father had been deported to Poland by the Nazis and was probably killed there; they assumed their mother was dead as well.

Again, we have become aware of a particularly striking case in which such a list has led to the reunification of a family. The refugee transport from Italy to Fort Ontario also brought six orphans, the Weinstein siblings. The oldest of the children, Marcella (Malka) Weinstein, had found the name of her long-assumed-dead mother on the list of refugees who had fled from France to Switzerland. The children had been separated from their parents after the total occupation of France by the Germans and had been able to get to Italy. They had heard that their father had been deported to Poland so they assumed the same about their mother. That's how the *Aufbau* unites families and friends – people who had given up all hope that their relatives and acquaintances are still alive. But the search work of the *Aufbau* only begins after the war

### Translation of a letter from the Rebbe Rayatz to Rabbi Tzebovol, mentioning the Shabbos parties Malka and Miriam Weinstein helped organize in Oswego, New York, 1944

B"H Monday 2nd of Elul 5704

Our dear and respected friend M.Y. Tzebovol

May peace and blessing be with you!

We've sent you a Siddur Torah Ohr, fifty copies of the Tehillim, and four sets of Mishnayos (two sets of Shas).

If some more copies of Tehillim are needed, please let us know and we will send some more, G-d willing.

Please currently strengthen the team of *Charedim*, in general, and Mr. Rothschild, in particular, so that they should sort out the reciting of the Tehillim publicly after the morning prayers, and according to Mr. Rothschild, you can definitely sort out the lecture of the Mishnayos as well.

We would like to know about the work of the committee for the "Shabbos parties" for girls, regarding the education of the girls Beth Rivka and Beth Soroh, the lectures for counselors, which is under the authority of his respected wife, the Rebbetzin, and also the hours of work so that we should be able to confirm the budget.

I'm sure you've received the two parcels of *Seforim* and booklets that Machane Yisroel and Mercaz L'inyonei Chinuch have sent you last week, and after further discussion regarding the reading material, we've decided not to send the above-mentioned *Seforim* to distribute them purposelessly, but to establish a library, which is open during fixed times for whomever wants to come there and read the *Seforim* and booklets, or to take them home on condition that they will be brought back after a period of time.

Translation of a letter from the Rebbe Rayatz to Malka and Miriam Weinstein, acknowledging their contribution to the Shabbos parties they helped organize in Oswego, New York, 1944

B"H 27th of Elul, 5704
Brooklyn

To the Rebbetzin Mrs. Rivka Mindel, president of the committee of the Shabbos parties in camp Oswego, and her assistants, Miss Malka Weinstein, Miss Miriam Weinstein, Miss Gittel Zigelman, and Miss Chava Dresner,

May G-d be with them.

May peace and blessing be with you!

I would hereby like to bless you and your parents and their families, with a blessing of *k'siva v'chasima tova*, may you have a good and sweet year, spiritually and physically.

I was happy to hear they've taken upon themselves the guidance matters regarding kosher education and to sort out the Shabbos parties you will strengthen yourselves to act and achieve with the right motivation, and blessings will land on your heads.

The one blessing them,

[signature]

## Translation of letter to Rabbi Moshe Tzebovol that mentions when Dovid Sussholz was attacked and almost killed by burglars.

To my dear friend R' Moshe Tzebovol and his wife, may you live to 120,

I've received today what you have sent me, many thanks for all that you have sent. Even though I've heard that all the people from Oswego camp have been freed, I saw from your address that you are still there.

Now I will continue writing in Yiddish, Mr. Schwartz from Lans [?] was in Switzerland, and he sent me regards from Moshe Bochner נ״י, He is doing very well, thank G-d. I'm sure you know he got married and lives in Switzerland now.

As of now there's no special news. Dovid and his wife, שיחיו, were here last week and they carried on traveling towards Belgium. He had, Heaven protect us, a misfortune in Italy; he was attacked by robbers. He already has his second child, *kein ayin hara*.

How is it going with you? I hope everything is perfect.

APPENDIX IV

# Weinstein Family Immigration Records in Antwerp, Belgium

Belgian law requires all foreigners to register their long-term stay at the town or city hall of the municipality where they reside, and to carry a valid residence permit during their stay. Upon registration, a national registration number is created. As Czech nationals, the Weinstein family had to register with the city of Antwerp. The following are documents from the city archives.

Chaim Yair (Jacob) Weinstein's national registration number 206486.
The family arrived in Belgium on April 10, 1928, and in Antwerp on April 11, 1928.

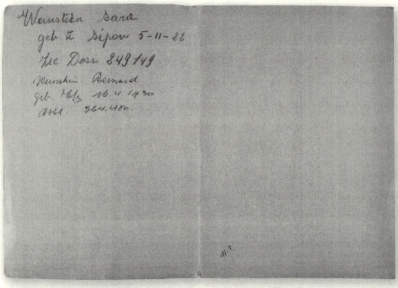

Sara Weinstein's national registration number 249149
Bernard Weinstein's national registration number 364480

# ANTWERP IMMIGRATION RECORDS · 239

*Chaim Yair (Jacob) Weinstein's registration, signed and dated May 21, 1929, listing his wife, Esther Perlman, and their children, Sarah, Malka, and Miriam, their current address as Leeuwerikstraat 44, Antwerp, and previous address as Kroonstraat 108, Borgehout, from April 15, 1928 to April 11, 1929. (Borgehout is a small district in the city of Antwerp.)*

*Chaim Yair (Jacob) Weinstein's registration, signed and dated November 11, 1934, stamped December 7, 1934, listing his wife, Esther Perlman and their children, Sarah, Malka, Miriam, Bernard, Etta, and Osiasz (Yankel), their current address as Wipstraat 47, Antwerp, and previous addresses as Leeuwerikstraat 29, Borgehout, from April 15, 1928 to November 11, 1932, and Bouwenstraat 18, Bourgehout, from November 19, 1932 to November 22, 1934. Identity card numbers are 1966 and 1967. Describes Jacob as a leader in the Jewish community, earning 240 francs weekly at Lange van Ruusbroecstraat 20, Esther as a housewife, and states that he provides for his wife and children. Family is given permission to live in Belgium for six months.*

*Chaim Yair (Jacob) Weinstein's family registration, signed and dated December 21, 1938, stamped December 22, 1938, listing his wife, Esther Perlman, and their children, Malka, Miriam, Etta, Osiaz (Yankel), Nathan (Naftoli), and Bertha (Gitel), their current address as Somerstaat 39, and their previous addresses as Leeuwerikstraat 29, Borgehout, Antwerp, from April 15, 1928 to November 29, 1932, Bouwenstraat 18, Borgehout, from November 29, 1932 to November 22, 1934, Wipstraat 47, Antwerp, from November 11, 1934 to April 5, 1938, and Kroonstraat 194, Borgehout, from April 5, 1938 to December 9, 1938. Identity card numbers are 65071 (Jacob) and 65072 (Esther), which are valid until December 22, 1939. Jacob's work permit, number 99659, is valid until February 28, 1940. Describes Jacob as a supervisor for the Israelische Gemeente, earning 250 francs weekly and Esther as a housewife. Family is given permission to live in Belgium for six months.*

*Nathan (Naftoli) Weinstein's birth certificate in
Jacob Weinstein's national registration file.*

*Berthe Gisèle (Gitel) Weinstein's birth registration
in Jacob Weinstein's national registration file.*

*Esther Perlman's registration as a foreign national, signed and dated December 2, 1946, listing her husband, Jacob (Chaim Yair) Weinstein, as deported by the Germans, and their children, Berthe Gisèle (Gitel) and David, their current address as Korte Van Ruusbroec 37, Antwerp. States that family left Belgium on May 13, 1940, because of the war to go to Montpellier, France. They stayed in a hotel in Nice until September 1943. Then they were in a family camp in Geneva, Switzerland, until October 1945, and another camp in Clarens, Switzerland, until November 13, 1946. They returned to Belgium on November 14, 1946. Supporting documents include her Czech passport, valid until December 31, 1946, and a visa. Describes Esther as not working, receiving 2,000 francs monthly from the Jewish community on Lange Leemstraat 155, Antwerp, and intending to remain in Belgium for more than six months. States that she will be issued an identity card, which will be valid until November 9, 1948.*

*Esther Perlman's registration, signed and dated September 10, 1959, listing her current address on Helenalei 18, Antwerp, with David Sussholz. States that her husband, (Chaim Yair) Jacob Weinstein, died in Germany, place and date unknown. Prior to her arrival in Belgium on July 16, 1959, her previous address was 210 Keap Street, Brooklyn, New York. States her plans to stay in Belgium until December 31, 1959 and that she is living with her daughter and son-in-law David Sussholz in an eight-room apartment on the third floor with her own room, and does not pay rent.*

*Esther Perlman's change of address registration, dated September 10, 1959, listing her address on Helenalei 18, third floor, which expires on February 10, 1950.*

*Registrar of national registration numbers, including Jacob (Chaim Yair) Weinstein's national registration number 206486.*

Made in the USA
Middletown, DE
27 July 2024

58067263R00156